GUERRILLA LOVERS

changing the world with
revolutionary compassion

VINCE ANTONUCCI

BakerBooks

a division of Baker Publishing Group
Grand Rapids, Michigan

Published by Baker Books
a division of Baker Publishing Group
P.O. Box 6287, Grand Rapids, MI 49516-6287
www.bakerbooks.com

Printed in the United States of America

Library of Congress Cataloging-in-Publication Data
Antonucci, Vince.
     Guerrilla lovers : changing the world with revolutionary compassion / Vince Antonucci.
         p.   cm.
     Includes bibliographical references (p.   ).
     ISBN 978-0-8010-6816-4 (pbk.)
     1. Christian life. I. Title.
BV4501.3.A578 2010
248.4—dc22   2009036971

10   11   12   13   14   15   16   7   6   5   4   3   2   1

To Dawson and Marissa—

You're the ones Jesus loves.
I pray that you would
know his love
and
ambush
the world
with
it.

CONTENTS

part 1

REVOLUTION

1

REVOLUTION CALLING

I'm about to do something dangerous. I'm going to bring you back to 1988. Guys, you may want to put on some parachute pants. Ladies, don't be caught in a shirt without shoulder pads.

Let me warn you that this is a land before boy bands. (People had no idea back then that the emptiness they sensed inside was a hole that only the New Kids on the Block could fill. Unfortunately for them, the New Kids would not dominate the charts until 1989. And those same people couldn't turn to the cheap substitute of Zack, A.C., and Screech on *Saved by the Bell* because, alas, it also arrived in 1989.)

1988?

It was an age of innocence, when we still believed in Milli Vanilli and silicone was more commonly found in cookware than women's breasts.

The year 1988 was when Bobby McFerrin sang, "Don't Worry, Be Happy."

Ironically, 1988 was also the year Prozac was introduced to the world. Apparently, Bobby McFerrin wasn't the answer for everyone.

If you turned on your TV in 1988, you might hear the theme song, "*Charles in Charge* of our days and our nights. *Charles in Charge* of our wrongs and our rights.*" This was a great concept—Scott Baio played a nineteen-year-old college student who gets hired to be the live-in nanny for a couple of hot young teenage girls. Shouldn't the song have gone, "*Charles in Charge* of our days and our nights (*bow-witcha-bow-wow*). *Charles in Charge* of our wrongs (*rrrowww*) and our rights"?

In 1988, if you fell and couldn't get up, you had no idea what to do, because those hysterical commercials with the old lady flopping around on the floor didn't start till 1989.

The commercial you *would* see in 1988 said, "This is your brain. This is your brain on drugs." Which made stoners everywhere say, "Dude, I could go for some eggs."

1988?

In 1988 a small group of power brokers so ruled the world that their influence was impossible to deny or resist. I speak, of course, of the California Raisins, whose dance moves mesmerized a nation.

The Beastie Boys could only sing about fighting for your right to party. Spuds MacKenzie actually lived it.

While Jessica Rabbit pursed her big, sexy lips, George Bush (H., not W.) was elected president by urging people to read his lips.

Teens sang along with "Parents Just Don't Understand" while moms and dads everywhere thanked Will Smith for reminding their kids that they just don't understand.

If you went to the movies, you might see the now governor of California as a bulging-muscled, steroid-popping twin ... to a guy who looked more like an Italian potbellied pig walking on two legs.

And it's certainly debatable, but perhaps the most important contribution made in 1988 was the new line Billy Ocean gave guys to use on the ladies: "Get outta my dreams, get into my car."

♥

I've taken you back to 1988 because it was a big year for me. I was graduating from high school. It was a turning point in my life. I was going to enter college and had to choose a major. It was a chance to examine myself. It was also a time to look back to see what I had learned through life and in school.

It wasn't pretty. Obviously some of it was good, but I felt like I couldn't see any good through all the crap.

In history classes I had learned of civil wars and world wars; genocides and suicides; people who wore swastikas and others who donned white hoods; crises in the Suez and with Cuban missiles; nuclear bombs and nuclear meltdowns; invasions by a Trojan horse and through a Bay of Pigs; Iran-gate and Watergate.

If that wasn't enough (and it was), I needed only to turn on the news to learn of the Iran hostage crisis and an AIDS epidemic; people dying from stepping on hypodermic needles on the Jersey Shore and from taking tampered-with Tylenol laced with cyanide; televangelists getting caught with their pants down and figure skaters getting their knees busted; Ethiopian children starving in Africa while American children received Halloween candy with razor blades concealed inside; war in the Middle East and a massacre in Tiananmen Square; political tensions between the USA and USSR and racial tensions between blacks and whites; space shuttle disasters and suicide bombers. It was true we no longer had Watergate, but we now had Whitewater. And all of this while Nancy Reagan was teaching us to "Just say no."

And if all that wasn't enough (and it *clearly* was), if I opened my door I learned firsthand of homelessness and latchkey kids; hearts broken by adultery and homes broken by divorce; illiteracy and illegitimate children; school bullies who tormented kids because their parents tormented them and school cafeteria monitors who tormented kids because they were tormented by their empty lives; child abuse, sex abuse, alcohol abuse, drug abuse—so many kinds of abuse I lost count.

Looking at all this, I couldn't take enough Prozac to ignore it, and I couldn't just smile and say, "Don't worry, be happy." No, something inside me screamed, *This can't be the way things are supposed to be! This is insane. It's ridiculous. Is it a joke? Is this the way it's always been? The way it will always be? Isn't anyone going to do anything? Something has to change.*

For as long as he could remember, he had been disillusioned with the world. Disillusioned with politicians who promised change, because nothing ever changed. Disillusioned with religious leaders who promised change, because nothing ever changed. Disillusioned with everyone who promised change, because *nothing ever changed.*

But something *had* to change. It was obvious. The world was a sleazy cesspool of inequity, corruption, and injustice. It was embarrassing to be a part of, to be associated with. And he wasn't just associated with it; he was forced to live in the squalor along with everyone else. It was like being stuck in a bad movie.

Somehow others could accept things the way they were. They could turn a blind eye, distracting themselves with trifling amusements. But not Nikki. He knew something had to change.

Eventually Nikki's disillusionment evolved into despair. Did they not have eyes? Were their minds so dull? How could all these people choose to live life in a gutter? Didn't they see the need for change?

His despair led him to heroin. The promise of escape was an offer he couldn't refuse. What started as an experiment soon became an addiction. Only when he was high could Nikki ignore what others so easily ignored. And since nothing ever changed, he decided to live life high.

But then the words came. Words he had been waiting to hear his entire life. Words that took his breath away as they breathed fresh life into his soul. Words that wrecked him and put his life on a new trajectory.

This was what he had been hoping for, yearning for, praying to a God he didn't believe in for: a revolution. There was a revolution calling.

Soon Nikki joined a secret organization led by a mysterious political and religious demagogue. This malevolent leader manipulated Nikki using a combination of his heroin addiction and brainwashing techniques. He turned Nikki into an assassin.

Okay, at some point I have to tell you none of this actually happened, which you know if you're a fan of late-eighties progressive metal. And if that's the case, you've probably identified this as the plot line from Queensrÿche's concept album *Operation: Mindcrime* (which came out in . . . 1988).

As the story progresses we learn that the revolution's leader, Dr. X, simply has to "speak the word" and he can get Nikki to do anything. The word is *mindcrime*. Nikki becomes Dr. X's pawn in a conspiracy to assassinate corrupt leaders. As a kind of twisted compensation, Dr. X offers Nikki the services of a hooker-turned-nun named Sister Mary. (This, of course, raises the question: What kind of services do hookers-turned-nuns supply? Are they sexual or spiritual? Perhaps they pray for you, but in all kinds of kinky positions? And do they wear low-cut habits? Does the church pay them by the hour?)

Nikki's friendship with Sister Mary eventually leads him to question his involvement in the nefarious plot of Dr. X. (Have you noticed how all relationships with hookers-turned-nuns have a positive impact on people? Hookers-turned-nuns have hearts of gold.)

Dr. X senses Nikki's wavering commitment to the mission, so he orders Nikki to murder Sister Mary. But Nikki can't bring himself to kill his hooker-turned-nun-with-a-heart-of-gold girlfriend. He goes back to Dr. X and explains that he and Sister Mary have decided to leave the organization. Dr. X then reminds Nikki that he is a heroin addict, and Dr. X is his supplier.

And so Nikki leaves feeling conflicted. What should he choose? Heroin or Sister Mary? Capital H or S.M.? The euphoria of "China white" snorted up his nose or that of a nun's lips pressed against his neck? Vows of assassinations, drugs, and rock 'n roll or vows of poverty, chastity, and obedience? Chasing the dragon or chasing the ex-hooker with the rosary beads? A nickel bag of smack or a night full of . . . prayer and contemplation?

When Nikki finally returns to Mary to tell her of his conversation with Dr. X, he finds her dead.

Nikki cannot deal with the loss, and considering the possibility that he may have killed her himself in a brainwashed state, he immediately goes insane. Right then the police arrive on the scene, arresting him for Mary's murder and the assassinations he committed for Dr. X. Nikki is overcome with grief and goes into a near-catatonic state. He ends up in a mental hospital.

So what do we learn from *Operation: Mindcrime*?

Well, for starters, if you are a hooker named Mary, chances are you will eventually become a nun. There are *no* ex-hooker nuns named Candy or Trixie. (Seriously, have you ever met a Sister Candy or Sister Trixie? Yeah, didn't think so.)

Second, if you are planning to join an evil cult that's plotting to take over the world, and you take the wicked cult leader's gift of a hooker-turned-nun as your girlfriend but think you may later question the wisdom of assassinating world figures, it's best not to be addicted to heroin. If heroin had a warning label, it would say:

Heroin has been known to impair the judgment of wannabe political radicals with hooker-turned-nun-with-heart-of-gold girlfriends.

And third: Everyone longs for revolution.

Nikki and I may feel the call more poignantly than others, but I believe every one of us hopes for, yearns for, and prays to God for change.

And if that's you, here's the good news: there's a revolution calling.

ANOTHER REVOLUTION?

Upon leaving high school I decided to major in political science and philosophy, figuring it might be a way I could be a part of changing the world. I discovered in my classes that the history of humanity is a history of revolutions. Want to see what I mean? Just search Amazon.com for "revolution" (you'll have over 460,000 books to choose from). Or google "revolution" (you'll get 186 million hits). Or Wikipedia wevolution. (Sorry, I had an Elmer Fudd moment there.)

Take *political revolutions*, for example, which have sought to overthrow an existing ruler or power. The French Revolution (1789–1799) had cataclysmic political implications. It came at a time of great upheaval as newly championed Enlightenment principles such as citizenship and inalienable rights forced people to reexamine the way they ordered life and government. The French Revolution was bloody and violent, featuring ten months known as the Reign of Terror, or in French, *La Grande Terreur*, which I thought was a drink at Starbucks. The revolution led to the overthrow of the

Bourbon monarchy in France and ultimately established the world's first republic (and, sometime thereafter, the world's first microwavable French bread pizza).

Then consider *social revolutions*, which have sought to change social structures. In South Africa a young man named Nelson Mandela saw a desperate need for change. Mandela was born into the Thembu dynasty, which reigns in the Transkeian Territories of South Africa's Cape Province. However, Mandela's great-grandmother was from the Ixhiba clan (called the "Left-Hand House"), and the descendants of this branch of the royal family were not eligible to succeed to the Thembu throne. (Just another example of The Man trying to keep the left-handers down. Fight the power, Southpaws!) Realizing that he would never hold local power and that a man with his skin color could not even vote nationally, Mandela sparked an uprising. This revolution certainly changed the political structure of that nation, but its goal was to bring about social change—the end of apartheid in South Africa, where being black reduced one to the status of a non-person. The revolution sought to end the social injustices of racial division and oppression that had stained South Africa for so long. Finally, on April 27, 1994, blacks were able to vote in democratic elections, and Mandela was elected president.

Often a revolution is both political *and* social. The Cuban Revolution began on July 26, 1953, when a troop of about one hundred poorly armed guerrillas attacked the Moncada Barracks. Many of the guerrillas were killed, but others were captured, including a young man named Fidel Castro. At the trial that followed, Fidel Castro spoke for *four hours* in his own defense. When a young upstart defends himself for four straight hours, you have on your hands either a future extremist dictator or a future used car salesman. Either way, Cuba's leader, General Fulgencio Batista, should have executed Castro immediately. He didn't. Instead he sentenced him to fifteen years in prison. After only two years Batista freed Castro and his comrades. Why? In large part because he was receiving pressure from the Jesuits. (The Jesuits belong to The Society of Jesus, which is a religious order of the Roman Catholic Church. Its members have been called "Soldiers of Christ," but this time, perhaps inadvertently, served as "Soldiers of Marx.") They managed to get Castro released. Fidel responded not by joining them on the mission field but by going into exile in Mexico, where he gathered other Cuban expatriates and trained to wage war in Cuba. When they were finally ready to attack, this rough group of outcasts returned to Cuba on a small boat named *Granma*. (I have a personal theory that their first choices, the *Pink Teddy Bear* and *Tinkerbell*, weren't available, so *Granma* was chosen in a close vote over the *Effeminate Florist*. I cannot prove this theory.) Soon Fidel Castro took over Cuba. Castro gained power politically and also began to implement social and economic changes, introducing Communist principles to Cuba.

Other notable revolutions we've heard of include Mao and the Chinese revolution, Lenin and the Russian revolution, Ghandi and his efforts in India, and the American Revolution. History records well over two hundred significant revolutionary movements.

Some revolutions make me laugh. I'm sure they weren't funny at the time, but the names of these revolutions are amusing. For instance, from 1835 to 1845, the "War of the Tatters." I don't know why I think that's so funny, but it sounds like a bunch of potatoes battling it out. (Names I would have preferred: "The Fracas of the French Fries" or "The Skirmish of the Spuds.") I can picture some elder statesman potato declaring, "There is a rumor going around that someday in the future people will cut us into batons, deep fry us, and cover us with chili and cheese. But we are, and always have been, a proud, starchy, and tuberous tribe. And I say to you today that this must never be!" But then some young hoodlum potato screams, "No, man, we *want* to go in the fryer! That is so extreme! Cover us with whatever, man!

Bring it on. We've got to fight for our right to partyyy!" And the battle was on.

In 1988 Estonians, Latvians, and Lithuanians overthrew their governments. The name? *The Singing Revolution.* I'd like to see video footage of that battle scene as the leader of the revolution steps up and belts out,

> O Estonia, I come to set you free.
> Latvia, you shall come to be with me.
> Lithuania, many men have loved you,
> But now you're mine
> Till the end of time.

Then his right-hand man yells, "Here comes our enemy!" and everyone takes dance positions and starts snapping their fingers.

In China in the first century AD, the (get this, I'm not kidding) *Red Eyebrow Rebellion* took place. Scene: a hilltop overlooking a river valley. A young man cautiously approaches a grizzled leader. Finally he gets his attention and says in an excited but hushed tone, "Hello. I want to join you. I will give my life for what you are setting out to achieve." The leader of the rebellion slowly looks him over, starting with his feet. Finally he gets to, and stares at, the young man's face. He opens his mouth and says, with deep regret, "I am sorry. It is true we need many more men, but you, my son—you do not have the red eyebrows."

The history of humanity is a history of revolutions.

Why?

Why so many revolutions?

I can imagine a world without revolutions. I can picture a history of humanity that's much more stable and accepting of the way things are.

So why so many revolutions?

I don't know for sure. But I have some suspicions.

First, I suspect that people share the same feeling as Nikki and I: something is wrong with the world. Don't you feel it? That something more, something better than what we're currently experiencing is available? It's like we have a splinter in our souls and are desperate to get it out. And when people feel that way, it's easy to blame the government or social or economic structures. People look at the world and realize that something is broken.

Second, I suspect people want to be a part of fixing it. Don't you? Now, part of this is altruistic; we want to make our world a better place. But making our world a better place also improves *our* lives. Our lives gain meaning and context as we get caught up in a story bigger than our own.

We all need that.

Why so many revolutions? Our world is broken and we want to be a part of fixing it.

♥

The revolutions never seem to cease. Around the world we continue to see revolution after revolution after revolution. And it makes me wonder if people are pointing the finger of blame at the wrong problems.

Maybe the world needs a different kind of revolution.

KINGDOM COME

It was the first century AD, and the Jews were anxious.

At the time Rome's kingdom extended from England to India. Movies today make ancient Rome seem rather sexy, but it was a ruthless empire that conquered the world by slaughtering hundreds of thousands of men, women, and children. Roman soldiers would enter a new town, put up a statue of Caesar, and command the people to bow down and worship. Anyone who refused would be massacred. Some accounts tell of thirty to forty thousand men, women, and children at one time being impaled on poles outside their hometown.

Once they established their authority, Rome taxed the people. An astronomical amount of money was required to fund Rome's massive army. Historians estimate the average Jewish household paid 90 percent of their income in taxes to Rome.

So the Jewish people, who believed they were called by God to be their own nation, were ruled by Rome's iron fist. And they were paying 90 percent of their income to fund the

Roman army, which had come in and killed scores of Jewish people and continued to oppress them.

All the elements were in place for a socially and politically explosive time bomb. A group of Jews called the Zealots violently opposed Roman rule over their Holy Land. Jewish factions repeatedly attempted insurrections against the Roman government.

But mostly the Jewish people yearned and waited. They longed for a kingdom all their own, and they waited for their leader. God had promised he would send a Messiah for his people. And the Jewish people ached for this Savior. They were sure that when he finally arrived, he would catalyze a rebellion against the kingdom of Rome; he would win them their political independence; he would lead them in a revolution.

Jesus's opening words were, "The time has come. . . . The kingdom of God is near. Repent and believe the good news!"[1]

One hundred and fifteen times the word *kingdom* is used in the Gospels. One hundred and eleven of those times it comes directly from Jesus's mouth.

These were, obviously, supercharged words.

Again, remember, a volatile cocktail of circumstances was mixing together to create an explosive situation. The Jewish people were on edge. Whispers of revolt, of an uprising, circulated widely. The people craved independence. They waited for someone to rescue them.

And then Jesus arrived.

He claimed to be the Messiah.

A desert prophet dressed in camel's hair with locust legs stuck between his teeth pointed at Jesus and said, "Here he is. This is the One we've been waiting for."

This Jesus seemed to match the description God had provided in days of old.

And he said, "The kingdom of God is near."

We don't speak of kingdoms today. Well, perhaps people do in Saudi Arabia, but in America it's almost a foreign term. But there is one kingdom we still speak of, one king we continue to recognize. His reign began very quietly on an otherwise uneventful December day. Not many noticed, though a few travelers did come to pay their respect. Before too long, however, people from all walks of life were calling him king. They continue to do so to this day.

I speak, of course, of the Burger King.

I enjoy an occasional trip to the home of the Burger King. But personally, I question his sovereignty. I mean, really, what is he the king of? Quarter pound slabs of ground beef? I ask you: Who made the Burger King king anyway? And is he really deserving of his royal status? I'll let you be the judge.

Fact number one: the two primary challengers to this "king's" throne are a *clown* and an *eight-year-old girl*. Hardly stiff competition.

Fact number two: McDonald's began in 1940 and Burger King in 1954, so yes, McDonald's did have a head start, but only by fourteen years. Yet today there are three McDonald's for every one Burger King. Wendy's began in 1969 (I must point out that this is also the year I was conceived), which was fifteen years *after* Burger King, but Wendy's has nearly caught Burger King for second place in the chopped beefsteak market share competition.

Fact number three: the Burger King lawsuit against Gene and Betty Hoots of Mattoon, Illinois. In 1952, Gene and Betty bought an ice cream shop from Gene's uncle Bill. The name of that ice cream shop? *The Frigid Queen.* (A variety of jokes could be told here, including some about my wife, your wife, and Hillary Clinton. I have decided not to go there. However, I do invite *you* to go there. Feel free to make up a *Frigid Queen* joke and write it here: _____

_____.)

The Hootses did so well selling frozen desserts, they decided to expand their business. They fixed up a two-car garage behind their ice cream shop as a place to sell hamburgers and French fries. When the time came to name their new establishment, they decided to play off of their neighboring *Frigid Queen* and call it *Burger King*. The year was 1959. Two years later, another Burger King came marching into Illinois, claiming dominion over the Land of Lincoln. Burger King opened a franchise in Skokie, then another in Champaign. By 1967 the chain had fifty Burger Kings in Illinois. It was time for the Hootses to defend their territory. Lawsuit followed countersuit followed lawsuit. Ultimately the courts decided that the Hootses had the Burger King name first in Illinois but the corporation had a nationwide trademark. The courts gave the Hootses a twenty-mile radius that the Burger King Corporation could not come into. So though Burger King may claim absolute sovereignty, the truth is that they have not, do not, and will never reign in or around Mattoon, Illinois.

And so I end by making this request: O alleged king of burgers, relinquish your crown, sir!

I say all of that to make this simple point: we don't speak of kingdoms today. It's almost a foreign term for us.

Jesus always used language and stories that were very familiar to his audience. *Kingdom* was an everyday term back then.

I wonder: if Jesus were to come and announce to us today what he had come to bring, what word might he choose? Perhaps he would say, "The time has come. The *dream* of God is near." Or maybe, "The time has come. The *mission* of God is near." Or, "The *network* of God is near." Or, "The *new economy* of God is near." I'm not sure, but I suspect that he would say, "The time has come. The *revolution* of God is near. Repent and believe the good news!"

Jesus came to bring revolution. And when he used the word *kingdom*, that is certainly what his Jewish audience would have heard. When Jesus said, "The time has come. The kingdom of God is near," heads snapped to attention, eyes got big, and people dropped what they were holding. They knew that with those words, Jesus was throwing down.

The time had come.

The revolution was on.

REVOLUTIONARY LEADER

Perhaps it surprises you to hear that Jesus threw down.

Perhaps you don't think of Jesus as a revolutionary leader, as a spiritual insurrectionist, as a divine insurgent, as a kingdom radical.

Somewhere along the line we have taken Jesus, the true Jesus who lived and breathed and walked the earth, and shrunk him into a caricature of himself. We've reduced him to a cute, cuddly character. The Bible says God made us in his image. We've remade Jesus in the image of, well, Elmo.

♥

Elmo is a popular, cute, cuddly character on *Sesame Street*. He is red and furry, has an orange nose, and is, according to himself, three and a half years old. In the mid-nineties Elmo's popularity soared. He became a regular guest on *The Rosie O'Donnell Show* and made appearances on *Martha*, *The Tony Danza Show*, *The View*, and, oddly, *The West Wing*.

Elmo also happens to be the only Muppet ever to testify before the U.S. Congress. (Take that, Miss Piggy!)

Elmo enjoyed a meteoric rise to fame, but not without incident. In 2006 some controversy arose over the book *Potty Time with Elmo*. The book featured buttons children could press, causing Elmo to say prerecorded phrases. Parents began to complain that one of the buttons led Elmo to say, "Who wants to die?" The book's manufacturer quickly explained that in fact, Elmo was saying, "Who wants to *try*?" It was the low quality of the sound chip causing the confusion. I, however, will always enjoy picturing Elmo growling, "Who wants to die?" In fact, I propose a new book, *Scarface for Toddlers: Starring Elmo!* which would feature Elmo saying wonderful phrases like, "You wanna play rough? Okay. Elmo wants you to say hello to Elmo's little friend," and "Elmo kill a Communist for fun, but for a green card, Elmo gonna carve him up real nice!" and "You think you can take Elmo? You need an army if you gonna take Elmo!"

Each of my kids went through a stage of being Elmo fans, so I had to be on a personal basis with Elmo for a while. I didn't enjoy much about that, but if pressed I'd say my favorite thing about Elmo is all the different versions of Elmo. I mean, Elmo is what he is—a cute, cuddly character—but there are some variations of Elmo. Though there is not yet a Scarface Elmo, there is Tickle Me Elmo. It's the cute, cuddly character, but he laughs if you tickle him. And there's Hokey Pokey Elmo (which, I've learned, is Hokey Cokey Elmo in the United Kingdom. Seriously? The Brits think the Hokey *Cokey* is what it's all about? No wonder they're so uptight!). Hokey Pokey Elmo is still the cute, cuddly character, but he puts his left foot in and his left foot out. There is also Limbo Elmo and Chicken Dance Elmo (which one time mysteriously sent me into an epileptic seizure). They're all just different versions of the cute, cuddly character.

I've been in a stage for a while now where I'm a pretty big Jesus fan. I'm on kind of a personal basis with him. I enjoy a lot of things about that, but if pressed I'd say my *least* favorite thing about Jesus is all the different versions of Jesus. I guess what I don't like is not anything about Jesus but what we've done with him. We have reduced Jesus to a cute, cuddly character, but we still also have some variations on Jesus.

Take Prozac Jesus. You see this version in almost every movie ever made about him. This version says that when he was here on earth, Jesus walked stoically through life, very detached and removed. He had a glassy look in his eyes, spoke with a slight British accent, and displayed no emotions.

Or Hippie Jesus. Hippie Jesus is laid back. He's always cool, calm, and collected. He came to bring peace to the earth. He wants everyone to get along and smile and be chill.

There's Mr. Rogers Jesus. This Jesus is kind of grandfatherly. He gives wise advice about life. He's very kind and sings, "Won't you be my neighbor?" He wears a yellow sweater and slippers and is so not-exciting that he can only be seen on PBS.

I don't believe any of these versions give an accurate picture of Jesus at all. In fact, when I, as a twenty-year-old, started reading the Bible for the first time, the Jesus I encountered was not cute or cuddly.

I met a revolutionary leader.

As I've mentioned, the first words Jesus spoke when he arrived on the scene proclaimed the kingdom he had come to establish. In that context, these were bold words that sparked thoughts of revolt and uprising. When people heard Jesus speak to them, they would have thought, "Finally we have a revolutionary leader!"

Later Jesus was invited to a meal at a Pharisee's house. The Pharisees were the religious leaders of the day, and for them it was all about religion—dressing right and acting right and talking right to keep the rules and impress the people. Jesus arrived for dinner, and the Pharisees were flabbergasted that he didn't wash his hands before dinner. Now, that may not have been very sanitary, but it wasn't unspiritual. Yet that's exactly what the Pharisees thought it was; they were ready to indict Jesus for breaking their religious rules.

Prozac Jesus would have very quietly apologized for making everyone upset and washed his hands. But the real Jesus did not apologize and did not wash his hands. Instead he said, "You Pharisees clean the outside of the cup and dish, but inside you are full of greed and wickedness. You foolish people! . . . You are like unmarked graves," and it just got worse from there.[1] Why didn't Jesus apologize and wash his hands? Because he *wasn't* Prozac Jesus. Why did he confront the hypocrisy of the Pharisees? Because he *was* a revolutionary leader.

Another time Jesus miraculously fed a gargantuan crowd of people with just a sack lunch. The next morning everyone came back, and why not? They found someone who provides a free meal, and they were hungry again. Jesus is better than Denny's! They asked for breakfast, and Hippie Jesus would have said, "Sure! I just want everyone to get along. If sharing a meal together is what you want, that sounds great. Let's just make sure we're all happy and peaceful. Let's sing, everyone! Kumbaya, myself, kumbaya . . ." But the real Jesus did not feed anyone and did not lead them in singing a wussy Christian chorus. Instead he refused to give them food and insisted (five consecutive times) that they must eat him. The Bible tells us that this was the day many decided not to follow Jesus anymore.[2] Why didn't Jesus provide breakfast? Because he *wasn't* Hippie Jesus. Why did he make such radical demands of his followers? Because he *was* a revolutionary leader.

On a different occasion Jesus walked into the temple where people were supposed to come near to God but people were in the lobby selling cattle, sheep, and doves at exorbitant prices. They were also unfairly exchanging money, taking advantage of people who had traveled there and would need an animal to sacrifice. Mr. Rogers Jesus would have very gently said,

"Now, I don't think you're being a very good neighbor. It might be nice for you to at least reduce your prices. You'd still make some profit, but it would help these other people out. Wouldn't that be the kind thing to do?" But the real Jesus did not promote a peaceful environment or kind business practices. Instead he made a whip and drove the greedy businessmen out of the temple, along with the animals they were selling. Why didn't Jesus simply provide some teaching on better business practices and explain that it's possible to be a capitalist and compassionate at the same time? Because he *wasn't* Mr. Rogers Jesus. Why did he pull the angry Indiana Jones routine on the merchants in the temple? Because he *was* a revolutionary leader.

In fact, think about this: Mr. Rogers was one of the most beloved people in the last few decades of American history. In the year he died, Mr. Rogers was the grand marshal of the Rose Bowl Parade. When he drove past the throngs of people, a great feeling of warmth came over the crowd. People smiled and waved and clapped for Mr. Rogers. Can you imagine if instead the crowd had pointed at Mr. Rogers and screamed, "Crucify him! Crucify him! Crucify him!"? Can you imagine some officials stripping off his cardigan and sandals, beating him to a pulp, nailing him to a cross, and leaving him to die? No, we can't imagine that, because that would never happen to Mr. Rogers. But that's *exactly* what happened to Jesus. Why? Because he *wasn't* a kind, cardigan-wearing grandfather. He *was* a revolutionary leader. You don't get crucified for being kind. You get crucified for being too radical.

And let's be clear: Jesus's life wasn't taken from him because he was too weak to stand up and defend himself. No, he died because he *chose* to lay down his life. Why? Because it was necessary to advance the revolution. He was strong enough to choose *not* to defend himself.

In fact, he was so strong that three days after laying down his life, he defeated death by walking out of his grave. We talk about that a lot on Easter, and we celebrate the "resurrection of Jesus," but we never really talk about the resurrected Jesus. That's a shame, because the picture we get of Jesus, post-resurrection, is definitely not of a cute, cuddly character but of a revolutionary leader. We get very brief glimpses of Jesus after his resurrection in the four Gospels and the book of Acts, but the main place we see the resurrected Jesus is in the book of Revelation.

In Revelation, Jesus is described as having eyes of blazing fire and the voice of rushing waters.[3] His face will burn your retinas if you stare at him too long.[4] He's sitting on a throne (remember, he came to establish a kingdom; he's the ruling king of that kingdom) and is surrounded by peals of thunder.[5] Finally he gets off the throne, and the reason is to fight. He's wearing a robe dipped in blood as he rides a white horse into battle, with armies following behind him.[6] He has a sword coming out of his mouth and is all tatted up on his legs, which proclaim "KING OF KINGS, LORD OF LORDS."[7] This is no G-rated scene; it's R-rated, and you definitely don't want your kids to watch. This has all the makings of a horror movie!

This is no cute, cuddly character. This is not emotionless Prozac Jesus, not pacifist Hippie Jesus, not "Won't you be my neighbor?" Mr. Rogers Jesus. This is Cowboy-Up, You-best-not-mess-with-him, I-just-saw-him-and-I-think-I-peed-my-pants, Ultimate Fighting Jesus!

This is the one we look to, call on, and call Lord, and it's not Elmo. Not even close.

Jesus is a revolutionary leader.

5

LOVE MARCH

The 2005 documentary *March of the Penguins* begins with the narrator saying, "In some ways this is a story of survival, a tale of life over death. But it's more than that, really; this is a story about love. . . . Like most love stories, it begins with an act of utter foolishness. The emperor penguin is technically a bird, although one that makes his home in the sea. So if you're wondering what he's doing up here on the ice, well, that's part of our story. Each year, at around the same time, he will leave the comfort of his ocean home and embark on a remarkable journey. He will travel a great distance, and though he is a bird, he won't fly. Though he lives in the sea, he won't swim. Mostly, he will walk."

As the movie continues, we learn that the walk of the emperor penguin is actually a march of love. He will travel seventy miles every year in temperatures ranging from 58 degrees to 80 below zero. The purpose of this march is to find a mate.

This leads me to believe that at some point the producers must have considered naming the movie *Penguin Booty Call*. Seriously, this is what the march of the penguins is—a seventy-mile, freezing, arduous, death-defying booty call. It makes me want to sit down with these penguins and say, "Listen, I totally respect your dedication to having sex. It is commendable. I mean, really, this type of devotion is typically seen only in desperate and misguided teenagers. I do have to ask, however: isn't there an easier way for you to copulate? I know the old adage about getting out of something what you put into it, so I imagine you're having the best sex on the planet. But still, can any sex be worth freezing to death over? I mean, couldn't an entrepreneurial penguin hire some hot female penguins and station one on each icy street corner? Put them in some stilettos, wrap hot pink boas around their necks, and you're in business."

But no, the penguins are apparently not a very enterprising group, and so they continue to make their march of love.

When most people think of Jesus, they think about the cross and how he died. And perhaps they think of Easter: how he rose from the grave. And so in some ways his is a story of survival, a tale of life over death. But when I first started reading the Bible I found that it is more than that, really; it's a story about love. In fact, if someone asked me to narrate the beginning of Jesus's life, I would have said, "Like most love stories, it begins with an act of utter foolishness. Jesus is technically God, and as God he makes his home in heaven. So if you're wondering what he was doing down here on earth, well, that's part of the story. At just the right time, Jesus left the comfort of his heavenly home and embarked on a remarkable journey. He traveled a great distance, and though he was preexistent, he was born. Though he lives in the skies, he won't fly. Mostly, he walked . . ."

As the story continues, we learn that the walk of Jesus is actually a march of love. That he will travel anywhere and under any circumstances, and his purpose was and is, in a sense, to find God a mate.

Now there was, obviously, nothing sexual about this journey. This was no booty call; it was a soul call. It was an expression of God's heart crying out to ours. It was God's passion traversing the land in sandals.

♥

This is what the people of Jesus's time couldn't understand. Remember, things were tense as the Jews lived under the hand of the Romans. The Jews were waiting for God to send a Messiah who would help them to establish their own self-ruled empire. And then came Jesus, and he said *kingdom*. And it was clear to anyone who spent time with Jesus or looked at his life that he was without question a revolutionary leader.

The problem was, Jesus came to bring a different kind of revolution.

It was not at all what people were expecting. It wasn't political, though it might at times have an influence on politics. It wasn't economic, though it probably should have some impact on economics. It wasn't social, though it can have social implications as well. The revolution Jesus came to bring was not primarily about politics or the economy or social structures. And this, as you might guess, disappointed the people. They had waited for and wanted a political, socio-economic revolution. And if you read through the Gospels, you'll see people assuming this was what Jesus came to do, hoping this was what Jesus came to do, and trying to push Jesus into doing just that.

But Jesus rebuffs all their efforts and instead simply continues his walk. Just as the penguins make their journey year after year, we see Jesus repeatedly making his march of love.

For instance, we read that Jesus "left Judea and went back once more to Galilee. Now he had to go through Samaria."[1]

This verse makes it sound like Jesus *had to go* because of geographical necessity, but that wasn't it. In fact, at the time the Jews and the Samaritans hated each other and would *never* enter each other's territory. Jewish people often made the trip from Judea to Galilee, but none of them took the direct route through Samaria. Instead they would take the long detour around the Sea of Galilee. All because they wouldn't be caught dead in Samaria. But Jesus, a Jew, "*had* to go through Samaria." Why? If it wasn't geography, what was it?

It was a woman. A certain woman in Samaria had made a mess of her life. She jumped from bed to bed to bed, which caused the men to love to use her and the women to love to hate her. She was living in guilt and shame, and she was continually going from man to man trying to address a void inside that no man could fill. So Jesus and his twelve buddies go into Samaria, and then Jesus sends them off to get lunch. I can picture the disciples saying, "Oh, so this guy can feed five thousand people, but he can't get his own sandwich? Nice, Jesus, really nice." But the true reason Jesus sent them off is because of the true reason he had to go through Samaria: he was on a march of love. He meets the woman, and they proceed to have a life-changing conversation. She had finally met a man who could offer her the love she'd been searching for all her life. This love would fill the emptiness inside of her and revolutionize her soul.

Another time Jesus and his friends get in a boat and start traveling across a lake to the region of the Gerasenes.[2] Soon a storm comes up, and chaos erupts. Waves are breaking across the boat. Jesus's guys, several of whom are professional fishermen, are screaming, "We're going to drown!"[3] The only course of action that makes sense is to turn around, but they don't. It's like Jesus *has to go* to the region of the Gerasenes. Finally they arrive. They stay there for only a short part of that day; only one thing happens during that time, and then they go straight back. On their way back the disciples must have thought, "Man, we nearly lost our lives to get there. Jesus was willing to risk everything for that one thing." So what was that one thing? It was a man whose life was in complete turmoil. In fact, he was considered so dangerous that he was kept locked up in a cemetery far away from town. *He* was the reason. Jesus was on a march of love. He met this man and brought order to his life as he removed what had been tormenting him. Jesus revolutionized this man's soul.

As a twenty-year-old with no prior knowledge of the Bible, I was the most shocked when I read John 3:16, which Christians seemed to take for granted (and post on signs at football games). I was stunned that "God so *loved* the world" that he sent his Son on a march of love from heaven to earth. And seemingly almost every chapter of the Gospels contained a story of Jesus loving someone others would have considered unlovable.

Jesus was the only sinless person who had ever lived, but he drew the most sinful people to him like a magnet.

Why?

Because Jesus was a revolutionary, but his was a revolution of love. Revolutions tend to be about changing the power in a certain geographical territory, but the only geography that concerns Jesus is that of a person's soul. Jesus came to bring a revolution of the heart.

Jesus came to offer a new way of living that flows out of a heart that's been transformed by God. He came to establish a kingdom that would start here on earth, would be located within each person who chooses to be a part of it, and would travel with them wherever they go. It's a countercultural kingdom offering an alternative way of life. This way of life is probably best summed up in the creed of Jesus.

REVOLUTIONARY CREED

I just found the coolest website. You enter a word, and this site generates an advertising slogan for it. You can even purchase a T-shirt featuring the slogan you created. I was thinking about this book, so I entered "revolution." The generator churned out "Have you had your revolution today?" I like it! Then I put in "guerrilla." The slogan? "You've always got time for guerrilla." Not bad! Next I submitted "lovers": "The loudest noise comes from the electric lovers." I don't know what that means, nor do I want to. Just for fun I typed in my first name and got "There's no wrong way to eat a Vince." Weird! Then my last name: "Go on, get your Antonucci out." Even weirder! Hoping for something really crazy, I typed in "sex," and it came up with, "Too orangey for sex." The odd thing is, I already have a shirt with that on it.

Advertising slogans are great because, ideally, they communicate something essential about the product. Apple Computers started out with the slogan "A computer in every home." At the time computers were very large, extremely expensive, and unbelievably complicated. With their slogan, Apple announced that they were going to design computers the average person could understand and afford. Or take Alka-Seltzer's motto, "I can't believe I ate the whole thing," which is kinder than the alternative, "We are the medication for fat, undisciplined men who suffer from the sin of gluttony. So when you finally get your head out of that plate of chicken wings, down a few Alka-Seltzers right quick!"

Sometimes advertising slogans get translated into another language and cease to communicate what was intended. Clairol introduced their "Mist Stick" curling iron into Germany only to find out that "mist" is slang for manure. Not too many people had use for a "Manure Stick," though I think they'd make great stocking stuffers. When Coca-Cola first introduced their product in China, they had no idea that their name translated into "Bite the Wax Tadpole." I can imagine the disappointment on the Chinese children's faces as they opened the red can to find it filled with a caramel-colored carbonated liquid rather than the hoped-for wax tadpole. Frank Perdue's slogan, "It takes a strong man to make a tender chicken," was translated into Spanish as "It takes an aroused man to make a chicken affectionate." Not what Frank meant to communicate, but nonetheless completely true.

Of course businesses are not the only source of famous slogans; political campaigns are another. While some have become renowned for their effectiveness or creativity, such as "I Like Ike," or "A Chicken in Every Pot. A Car in Every Garage," others, well, not so much. For instance, in the 1884 US presidential campaign, Grover Cleveland used the slogan, "Blaine, Blaine, James G. Blaine. Continental Liar from the State of Maine." No one can deny that it rhymes, but this is the best his staff could create? And what exactly is a continental liar? (I don't know, but I have been called the Continental Lover.) But my favorite campaign slogan of all time came from then president William McKinley, running for reelection in 1900 with the slogan, "Leave Well Enough Alone." Not, "We're Moving in the Right Direction!" or "Honor Excellence!" or even "Don't Mess with Success." No, it's "Leave Well Enough Alone." McKinley told the nation, "By no means do I think I'm doing a great job, but hey, can't we settle for known mediocrity over the unknown?"

Revolutions often have slogans too, though they're more typically referred to as creeds. In fact, one of the best ways to understand a revolution is to look at its creed. One example is the American Revolution, where the battle cry was "No taxation without representation." With that simple statement people living in America declared, "You can't rule us and take our money without giving us a say in the government." Or Ho Chi Min who, in leading a revolution against the occupying French government in Vietnam, would repeatedly say, "It is better to sacrifice everything than to live in slavery." From that one sentence I understand what drove Ho Chi Min and the Vietnamese people and what they were setting out to achieve.

If Jesus came to lead a revolution, did it have a creed? Yes.

Jesus gave a motto that helps us to more fully understand the nature of his revolution. He gave it in response to a question.

Jesus was in a debate with some religious scholars when he was suddenly interrupted. "One of the teachers of the law came and heard them debating. Noticing that Jesus had given them a good answer, he asked him, 'Of all the commandments, which is the most important?'"[1]

Perhaps this teacher of the law was trying to trap Jesus, hoping Jesus might give a bad answer and be exposed as a false teacher. Or maybe this was a question this teacher had wrestled with himself, and seeing wisdom in Jesus, he wanted to hear Jesus's opinion. Or could it be that this teacher of the law heard the good answers Jesus was giving? He looked around and realized that large and growing crowds of people were listening, nodding, and smiling at Jesus's words. He recognized that this was quickly becoming a revolution, and it was gathering momentum. So he wanted to know: What is going on here? What is Jesus really communicating? What does he want people to do? What is this revolution all about?

We don't know the motivation for the question, but we do know Jesus's answer. "'The most important one,' answered Jesus, 'is this: 'Hear, O Israel, the Lord our God, the Lord is one. Love the Lord your God with all your heart and with all your soul and with all your mind and with all your strength.' The second is this: 'Love your neighbor as yourself.' There is no commandment greater than these.'"[2]

Jesus gave words for the heart of what he was doing. He provided his revolution a creed, a motto, a battle cry. And if you boil it down to its essence, it's "Love God. Love people."

More is actually going on with Jesus's response than meets the eye of the modern reader. Jesus does not pull this creed out of the air.

The Jewish people had a creed of their own. It's called the Shema. For centuries prior to Jesus's time, and even up to today, the Shema is the first prayer taught to Jewish children. Observant Jewish people recite the Shema when they wake and before they go to sleep. Every Jewish synagogue service begins with the words of the Shema.

The Shema is made up of three Old Testament Bible verses. The first is from Deuteronomy 6, the second from Deuteronomy 11, and the third from Numbers 15. The Shema begins by quoting Deuteronomy 6:4–5: "Hear, O Israel: The LORD our God, the LORD is one. Love the LORD your God with all your heart and with all your soul and with all your strength." The second and third parts of the Shema are about obeying God.

So Jesus is asked for his creed, and he begins by reciting the Jewish creed, the first part of the Shema. And the people listening would have nodded their heads in agreement. *Yes, we are Jewish; Jesus is Jewish; he is reciting our creed. This is all very good.*

But then Jesus leaves out the second and third parts of the Shema and attaches to the first part his own new addition, quoting Leviticus 19:18, "Love your neighbor as yourself."

Shock waves must have gone through the crowd. Can you imagine? It would be like if I was asked to lead both houses of Congress in saying the Pledge of Allegiance before a special joint session. So I took the stage, stepped to the microphone, and said:

> I pledge allegiance
> to the flag
> of the United States of America
> and to the Republic
> for which it stands
> which is a whole lot of crazy partying with Colt 45
> and pork rinds!

You don't just go and change the creed of a people. But that's exactly what Jesus did. The creed he taught that day was old but new. It was still all about loving God, but it was now also about loving people.

After Jesus changed the Jewish creed and gave his own, there must have been a stunned silence for some time. And the teacher of the law must have been tempted to just sneak away or to publicly rebuke Jesus so that no one would associate him with Jesus's radical words. But he didn't. Instead he said, "You are right in saying that God is one and there is no other but him. To love him with all your heart, with all your understanding and with all your strength, and to love your neighbor as yourself is more important than all burnt offerings and sacrifices."[3]

Jesus must have smiled.

Then Jesus opened his mouth again and said, "You are not far from the kingdom of God."[4]

Isn't that interesting? Jesus doesn't say, "You have a good philosophy of life," or "I'm glad you agree with me," or "You're a good student of the Scriptures." No, Jesus says, "Hey, look at you! You're not far from the *kingdom of God.*"

Why?

Because that's what love God, love people is all about. It's all about the kingdom of God. It's all about the movement Jesus came to lead. It's the creed of the love revolution.

I just put "love revolution" into the advertising slogan generator. It came out with "Happiness is a cigar called love revolution."

Huh?

I put it in again.

This time it said, "Splash love revolution all around."

That's more like it. And that's what Jesus was asking us to do when he announced his revolutionary creed: Love God. Love people. Splash the love revolution all around.

CONTAGIOUS LOVE

Jesus came to establish a kingdom, to ignite a revolution.

We learn a lot about that revolution by studying the life of its founder. What was Jesus known for?

Love.

He loved people no one else would love. His love was so radical, it restored souls and turned lives upside down. Time and time again, Jesus made the march of love.

We learn more about the revolution by examining its motto. Jesus lived before the time of Madison Avenue and Christian bookstores, so his slogan was not screamed by salesmen on TV commercials, nor was it printed on cheesy T-shirts, pens, or mints. Even still, his revolution had a creed: Love God, love people.

But that's not enough detail for my Ginsu knife–sharp intellect. I have a *National Enquirer*, inquiring-minds-need-to-know desire for more about this revolution. So what is the kingdom of God really like?

Fortunately, Jesus once posed that exact question. He said, "What is the kingdom of God like? What shall I compare it to? It is like a mustard seed, which a man took and planted in his garden. It grew and became a tree, and the birds of the air perched in its branches."[1]

Jesus loved to tell ordinary-sounding stories that had a spiritual point. And almost always these stories had at least one element of surprise.

Remember, Jesus took center stage with the words, "The time has come. The kingdom of God is near." One hundred eleven times the Bible records Jesus saying the word *kingdom*. And now he asks, "What is the kingdom of God like? What shall I compare it to?"

A mustard seed.

Surprise!

When a mustard seed grows it becomes a weed. It's a vine-like weed which will grow and grow and will intertwine with other weeds.[2] And they'll continue to grow. And then they'll come into contact with a flower, which will be overtaken by the weeds. Now they're growing more. Soon they'll touch a tomato plant, and pretty soon that tomato plant has been overtaken by the weeds.

In fact, Jewish law at the time of Jesus made it *illegal* to plant mustard seed in a garden. Why was it against the law? Because they knew that it would grow and grow, invade the vegetables and other plants, and eventually take over the garden. If you let mustard in, eventually you'd be left with only mustard. The secret to gardening for the Jewish people of Jesus's day was: keep the mustard out!

I wonder how people reacted when they heard Jesus compare his kingdom to mustard seed planted in a garden. Did they just look shocked? *Are you serious? Don't you know about mustard?* Or did they giggle? *This guy is hysterical. I can't wait to hear what he's going to say next!* Or perhaps they frowned and thought, *Jesus, hush. We like you, and if you keep comparing your kingdom to mustard, you're going to get yourself killed.*

Jesus used a notorious, forbidden weed to describe God's kingdom. He said God's kingdom is like a man who planted a mustard seed in his garden. But people *didn't* plant mustard seed in gardens. It was illegal. If you did, the mustard seed would grow and grow and take over the entire garden.

I've tried to think of modern-day equivalents. If Jesus was here today and asked, "What is the kingdom of God like? What shall I compare it to?" what would he say next? What modern-day metaphor would make the same point and have similar shock value?

Maybe: "What is the kingdom of God like? What shall I compare it to? It is like a vicious computer virus a man sent out in an email from his computer, and it spread and spread and infected more and more and more computers."

Or perhaps this: "What is the kingdom of God like? What shall I compare it to? It is like AIDS, which infected one person but soon spread and spread and became an epidemic as scores of people received it."

If we heard that, our heads would spin. We'd say, "What? Are you serious?" And the people who heard Jesus back then would have reacted the same way.

♥

So what was Jesus trying to teach us about the kingdom of God?

The Jesus revolution is subtle. It starts small, like a weed in a garden, but it spreads. It reaches out, and everything it touches it grabs and pulls in. It spreads one life to another, more and more people getting pulled into it. And the harder you try to get rid of it, the faster it spreads.

I think Jesus is teaching us that the revolution is meant to be viral. It spreads like a disease. It's a disease you *want* to catch, but still it spreads like a disease. When you hang out with someone who has the flu, you catch the flu. Jesus is saying the revolution should be *sneezable*. The revolution should be contagious, and when it comes into an area, it should grow into an *epidemic*.

But it will only grow into an epidemic if it's done right. Weeds don't come in and announce they're taking over the garden. They don't invite all the other plants and vegetables to a meeting and ask them if they'd like to be taken over by the weeds. They don't hand out tracts explaining the benefits of a garden overrun by weeds. They don't wear weed T-shirts. They don't put a billboard up for all the vegetation to see: "For the Gardener so loved the garden, he gave his one and only weed."

No, a weed comes in unannounced, popping up very subtly, and it starts to grow. Then another weed pops up. And if these two weeds meet up, they'll get enmeshed, and then they'll intertwine with another weed. Soon they're pulling in flowers and plants, and eventually the entire garden is taken over by the weeds.

And Jesus teaches us that this is the way of his kingdom. The way his revolution is intended to function, the way it grows best, is not through public meetings, billboards, and TV. No, it's a love revolution that spreads person to person, one individual to another. And when we try to make it something it's not, it just won't work quite right. But when we live it out as it's supposed to be, watch out.

♥

Until 311 AD Christianity was illegal. If you became a Christian, you knew you were inviting persecution, perhaps death. If you talked about Christianity openly, you would be persecuted and probably killed. Until 311 AD there were no church buildings, no public church services, and no officially licensed pastors. Early Christians had no Christian radio, no Christian TV, and no Christian websites. There were no Christian bumper stickers and no Christian T-shirts. They didn't even have the Bible put together yet to give to people!

Now consider that in 100 AD the Christian population of the world was about twenty-five thousand. How much do you suppose Christianity spread between 100 AD and 311 AD?

The number of Christians went from twenty-five thousand to *twenty million*.

♥

Prior to 1941 about two million Christians lived in China. But then Mao Tse-tung captured power. Mao hated religion, perhaps especially Christianity. Upon taking over, Mao made Christianity illegal. He banished all foreign missionaries. He took away all church property. He killed the senior leader of every church and killed or imprisoned the second and third leaders of every church. He banned Bibles and all public meetings of Christians. Throughout his reign the government persecuted Christians whenever they sniffed them out.

People wondered what had happened to Christianity during Mao's reign, assuming that it probably had died out. When he died in 1976, they finally had the chance to find out.

What they learned was that in those thirty-five years, Christianity in China went from two million to *sixty* million.

♥

How did Christianity experience such explosive, exponential growth in the first century AD and under Mao's rule in China?

Before we answer that question, we need to contrast those situations to what's happening now in the United States. For us, Christianity is legal. We have church buildings, public church services, Bibles, professional leaders. We have Christian TV, books, radio, and websites to help "spread the Word." We have Christian T-shirts, bumper stickers, and breath mints (filled with Christian Retsyn!). So how quickly is Christianity growing in America? Well, it's not. The number of Christians is decreasing steadily and rapidly. By some accounts the percentage of Christians in America went from about 40 percent to 16 percent in the last few decades. So how do we explain the exponential growth of Christianity?

Jesus already did. His is a mustard seed revolution. It's plants popping up in a garden and then taking over the garden. One pops up and touches someone else with God's love, and that person has the evil and the hate choked out of them, and they're overtaken by the love revolution, and then those two band together and they touch someone else, and the bitterness is choked right out of them by God's love, and they join the revolution, and they touch someone else, and the empty life is choked right out of them as they're overtaken by God's love. Jesus's love revolution spreads person to person, from one individual to another.

This is the way I've seen the love revolution spread from my own life. When I first became a Christian, back in college, I was working about 25 hours a week at a movie theater. I quickly realized I was the only Christian working there. So I decided to take over the theater. That's what a weed does when it pops up in a garden. It doesn't whine. It doesn't say, "I want to go to a garden that already has weeds in it." So I tried to live a revolutionized life and really love God and love people.

A guy named Bill found out I was a Christian and cursed me out. Big time. He hated Christians. But I just kept loving him, even when he yelled at or threatened me, and eventually I got him to a point where he didn't hate Christians anymore.

Another guy at the theater was named Ryan. Ryan was a short, body-building Chinese guy with hair down to his butt. Ryan was mean. I was out of town the week Ryan started work, but when I returned I learned that he had already threatened to beat several people up. He would stare at a person and then break a broom over his leg. No one wanted to be paired up with Ryan, so I volunteered. And I decided to be nice to Ryan regardless of how mean he was to me. After months of us working together, graduation rolled around. I was graduating from college and about to enter law school at the University of Illinois. Ryan was graduating from high school and planned on attending college at Miami of Ohio. I discovered that Ryan wouldn't have a car at college, so I asked him if he'd like me to pick him up and drive him home for holidays.

Ryan asked, "You'll drive from Illinois to Ohio to pick me up, and then drive me to Buffalo?"

"Right," I answered.

He asked, "How far is that?"

"I have no idea," I admitted.

He said, "What if it's ten hours from your school to mine, and then another seven to Buffalo?"

"Well," I responded, "I'll have a seventeen-hour drive then, won't I?"

Ryan looked incredulous. "You'd really do that for me?"

I laughed and said, "Of course."

A few months later, on one of those seven-hour drives from Oxford, Ohio, to Buffalo, New York, Ryan decided to give his life to Jesus. He got pulled into the love revolution.

This is also the way I've seen the love revolution spread at my church, Forefront. Seven years after I decided to start following Jesus, he led me to start a new church in Virginia Beach. We started about eleven years ago with four people but have since grown to hundreds. We do some advertising to bring people in, but whenever we do surveys and ask people what brought them to Forefront, 80 percent say, "A friend." When I ask people, "What brought you to Forefront?" the answers I get time and time again are "Well, I know this person who comes," "Man, this person at work has changed so much since they started coming here, I had to come and see what it was about for myself," and "My neighbor is just so great, she does so much for us, so when she asked me to come I had to say yes."

One of my favorite examples of this is a young lady named Sarah. Sarah was a single mom with a good job and a decent life, but she still felt like something was missing. She knew some Christians, and they seemed different. They made her wonder if maybe what she was missing was God, if there even was such a thing as God. One day she was working out at the gym and confessed to someone that she had been wondering about God. The person said, "You should talk to the lady who works at the reception desk. She's a Christian and she *loves* her church." So Sarah asked the receptionist what church it was, and the lady responded, "Forefront! You should go!" Sarah decided to give it a try.

She was very nervous walking in her first Sunday but was surprised to see someone she worked with standing in the lobby. She walked over, and her coworker greeted her and said, "Evan from work goes here too! He's in the auditorium right now." So Sarah walked into the auditorium. At that moment our band was starting to play, and Sarah stared at them in confusion. Then she realized why they looked so familiar. Sarah waitressed for extra money, and the Forefront band played in her bar each month. Sarah sat down and really enjoyed the service. The guy speaking (a wildly sexy dude named Vince Antonucci) mentioned the importance of doing our spiritual journey in community and how everyone should get in one of Forefront's small groups. Sarah thought, "That does sound good. But I don't need a Forefront small group. My neighbors host some kind of Bible study group at their house. I trust them; I'll go to their group."

That afternoon Sarah walked next door and asked her neighbors if she could start attending their small group. They said of course; she thanked them and then, before walking away, asked, "By the way, what church do you go to?" They answered, "Forefront." Tuesday night Sarah showed up, and the first person she saw was one of her best friends from years earlier. A couple months later I watched Sarah being baptized, and I could picture these vines grabbing Sarah from every side. She got pulled into the love revolution.

Jesus's revolution is about mustard. (Surprise!) It's a weed that pops up and takes over a garden. It's a virus that can infect anyone in its path and turn the world upside down. It's a sneezeable revolution that anyone can catch . . . if, and only if, it's spread by a contagious love.

part 2

GUERRILLA

GUERRILLA LOVEFARE

Becky sat in the driver's seat of her car, trying not to be noticed. The sun wasn't up quite yet. No one would be coming out of their houses, and even if they did, they probably wouldn't be able to see her. But she hunkered down just in case. She couldn't believe it had come to this. From the beginning she had assumed it would go somewhere, but not here. She had never done anything like this; the thought had never crossed her mind. But now she had to go through with it. And she knew he would be there any minute. She had to be ready. *I can't believe I'm going to do this. I can't believe I'm going to do this. I can't believe I'm going to do this.*

It's about revolution. It's about splashing the kingdom of God all around. Generally I'm not one for war imagery and war metaphors, but it's difficult to ignore the connotation when you're talking about a "revolution."

I am not an expert on warfare, but it seems to me there are two basic ways to engage in a modern-day war. One is *shock and awe*. This is when the balance of power is on your side, so you move in the troops, roll in the tanks, and drop bombs from above. The goal is to rapidly destroy your enemies and force them into quick submission.

I wonder if, as Christians, we've relied on "shock and awe" tactics too much. We've tried to attract people to Christianity through our big church buildings, slick presentations, cool music, and quality programs.

The other way is *guerrilla warfare*. Guerrilla warfare is a method employed when you're outnumbered by the opposing force. Guerrilla warfare relies on intelligence. You must outthink the enemy.

It also relies on espionage. You must know your opponents, being able to discern where they are, how they think, and what they'll do next.

Guerrilla warfare features strategic surprise attacks. You must hit your opponents when they're not expecting it. These ambushes are usually low-intensity, close-proximity confrontations. You don't have the firepower to blast away from a distance, so you sneak up close, hit 'em quick, and get out of there.

I admit this metaphor breaks down quickly because those we're trying to reach are not our opponents or enemies. They are the people Jesus loves, and we're bringing his love to them. But you get the point. Jesus didn't call us to use shock and awe; he called us to use guerrilla tactics.

It's time to do the kingdom of God the way Jesus taught. It's time to be mustard seeds that pop up as weeds in a garden and then slowly, subtly take over the garden. It's a guerrilla revolution. And it's a *love* revolution, so we are to wage guerrilla *love*fare. The best way to attract people is through how we live and love.

We are guerrilla lovers.

In the last chapter we looked at how the original church experienced explosive growth between 100 and 311 AD. Why did it grow so rapidly? Historians who study this suggest two decisive influences. Both of these were . . . *plagues*. Not what you expected? Typically, widespread death-bringing epidemics don't add to anyone's "attendance" numbers, but historians tell us that Christianity grew rapidly in part because of these two horrific plagues. And they were horrific. In some cities, two-thirds of the population died. At the height of one of these plagues, in 251 AD, five thousand people were dying every day.

When the plagues came, everyone fled the cities to avoid the lethal contagion—everyone, that is, except Christians. The Christians stayed and ministered to the sick and dying. Dionysius, then Bishop of Alexandria, wrote of how the Christians responded to the plague of 250 AD. He explains that they

> showed unbounded love and loyalty, never sparing themselves and thinking only of one another. Heedless of danger, they took charge of the sick, attending to their every need and ministering to them in Christ, and with them departed this life serenely happy; for they were infected by others with the disease, drawing on themselves the sickness of their neighbors and cheerfully accepting their pains. Many, in nursing and curing others, transferred their death to themselves and died in their stead.[1]

These first Christians knew they had joined not a religion but a revolution. They knew they could not add others to the revolution with power, so they did it through the way they lived their lives. They became guerrilla lovers. They knew they could catch something and die, but they hoped those to whom they ministered would also catch something—the love of Christ—and live eternally. They chose to be people offering contagious life in a place filled with contagious death, and because of that decision, the revolution spread.

A few years after meeting Jesus and joining the revolution, I decided to go into full-time ministry and then to start a church. When we started the church I had virtually no experience as a pastor. We moved to a town where we didn't know a single person. The odds were completely against us.

It was perfect.

We had no choice but to get guerrilla.

We selected our name—Forefront: A Church to Turn the World Upside Down—and we chose our mission/purpose/vision statement: *Love God. Love People.* And from day one we taught our people that we were part of a revolution and that we were to be guerrilla lovers.

We wanted to destroy the negative stereotypes people have of Christians and of church. We wanted to make the "Good News" look and sound and feel good again. And we were willing to do anything (other than sin) to help people encounter Jesus and find life in him.

We started feeding homeless people at a shelter and volunteering at a local orphanage. We built a medical clinic in Haiti. We challenged our small groups to find creative ways to serve the community. One time my group landed on the idea of cleaning the bathrooms of local businesses and restaurants. So we gathered a bunch of cleaning supplies and launched out in pairs. The car I was in stopped at a Taco Bell. We explained to the manager that we wanted to scrub the bathrooms, for free, as a service to them. He seemed very perplexed by it all, but he agreed. I volunteered to clean the men's room by myself. It was the worst mistake I have ever made. I walked into the bathroom, put on my gloves, bent down by the toilet, and suddenly "MexiMelt" took on new meaning. Pretty soon I was using *gordita* as a curse word. This happened seven years ago, and I have not eaten in a Taco Bell since. To this day I can't hear the word *chalupa* without throwing up in my mouth a little.

On a Sunday morning in 2001 we asked everyone (without warning) to leave their shoes behind so we could donate them to homeless people. That led one couple to start bringing lunches down to the beach for homeless people, which soon blossomed into a full-on homeless ministry. Seeing the love of our people for the homeless and the life change it was causing led someone to donate a mobile home, hoping it could be used to get a family off the streets. This led dozens of Forefronters to donate their time to completely renovate it. Finally we were able to present a redone mobile home to a single mom and her son. This led someone else to donate a second mobile home. We completely renovated that one and presented it to another family. This led to our receiving a third mobile home and getting another family off the streets. This trailer park now has sparkling mobile homes with families in them who are beginning to experience and grasp the grace of God. It's like weeds popping up in a garden (or, actually, like flowers popping up in a garden of weeds).

And it's been contagious in all kinds of ways. I was at one of the presentations of a mobile home to a family. The director of our homeless ministry mentioned to me that a neighbor was admiring the swing set our church had put in for the family. This single mom had explained that she was saving up for a swing set like that one for her three children to play on. She had saved most of the money, and once her tax refund came in, she'd be able to purchase it. I told the director, "Tell her not to worry about it, that one of the small groups from our church will buy it for her."

"Really?" he asked.

"Yeah," I told him. "My group will do it."

He said, "Cool, but you tell her."

I said no, but he insisted, and pretty soon he had me standing in front of the neighbor. He explained to her, "This is the pastor of my church. He wants to tell you something."

"Well, I heard that you were saving up for a swing set," I began. "Why don't you keep the money you've saved? My small group will buy a swing set for you and install it."

She seemed confused, giving me the same look she might have if a family of groundhogs had crawled out of my nose,

announced it was a Led Zeppelin cover band, and started singing, "Whole Lotta Love." She said, "I don't understand."

"We just like doing nice things for people . . . because,
well, that's what God is like, and we like to be like him," I
explained. "So we'll buy you the swing set."

"But . . ." Huge tears started spilling down her cheeks. "I
don't understand. No one's ever . . . done anything like this
for me. Are you *really* gonna do this for me?"

"Yes. Really."

She was now in full sob. "Thank you so much. I just—I
don't understand. Thank you so much." She ran off to tell
her kids.

That was one of the best moments of my life.

Our church has always tried to be like that. We've always
practiced guerrilla lovefare. At one point we decided to try
something to spark people who perhaps hadn't caught on
yet. We handed everyone a sealed envelope on their way in
to our service several Sundays in a row. At the end of each
week's service we explained that these were guerrilla lover
assignments for them to complete in the next seven days.
This led to an outbreak of people ordering pizzas for their
neighbors, dropping cookies off at fire departments, mowing lawns for old ladies in the neighborhood, buying lunch
for the person behind them in the drive-through, cleaning
the bathroom at their office, tipping the dishwasher in the
restaurant, and much more. Just about everyone completed
their guerrilla lover assignment each week. Many continued to do guerrilla lover assignments even after we stopped
providing them.

♥

That's why Becky was sitting in her car that morning.

Becky was one of the people who completed her guerrilla
lover assignments but then decided to continue doing them
on her own. She began to think creatively about how she
could ambush people with God's love.

So one morning she got up early, baked chocolate chip cookies, went out to her car, slouched down in the seat, and waited nervously. She's not sure why she was so nervous, but she was.

Finally he showed up: the garbage man. As he drove up to her trash can, she sprang out of her car, ran up, and handed him the plate of warm cookies. The garbage man was stunned. He stuttered out a thank-you, explaining that no one had ever done anything for him before. Becky, not knowing quite what to say, blurted out, "Well, I'm a guerrilla lover."

Becky says she couldn't wipe the smile off her face all day. People at work kept asking what she was so happy about. At first she said, "Nothing, you wouldn't understand." But finally they got it out of her. She explained what she had done and how it was maybe the most joy she had ever experienced.

One coworker approached Becky later and asked, "Could I please come to church with you this Sunday?"

Becky was shocked and asked why.

"Well, I don't know," her coworker shrugged. "I want to be a part of something like that."

Becky said sure, and her coworker joined her that Sunday.

The next week person after person came up to Becky to tell her that they'd heard how great her church was.

The following Sunday Becky had an entire row of coworkers with her.

Being guerrilla is contagious, and that's what we are.

We're guerrilla lovers.

We practice guerrilla lovefare.

It's Time to Talk Guerrilla

Most of the chapters from now on will end with a list of questions. They can help you to dive deeper into and apply the ideas in the chapter, or, even better, you can use them to generate discussion with a group of your friends. Some of the questions will be based on short Bible passages. So if you don't have a Bible, um, well, maybe you should go get one.

1. How did you feel after reading the story about Becky?
2. What struck you most about that story? Was it (a) how easy it was to make someone's day, (b) that the garbage truck driver had never had anyone show him that kind of love, (c) how it made Becky feel to engage in guerrilla love, (d) the reaction of her coworkers, or (e) something else?
3. This chapter mentioned that Christianity grew exponentially in the early years through Christians loving people beyond reason in the face of two horrible plagues. What kind of plagues exist today that Christians can love people through? How could you personally do this?
4. Read Ephesians 2:4–10. The passage begins by mentioning God's love toward us, his grace toward us, and his kindness toward us. It is because of God's love, grace, and kindness that he sent Jesus and we can now be made alive in him. How are you doing at accepting and applying God's love, grace, and kindness in your life?
5. The passage then says that we are not saved by our good works, but once we have allowed Jesus to save us, we are to do good works. Why do you think so many people get the order confused and try to do good works to earn God's favor, rather than doing them as a grateful response to God's favor?
6. Verse 10 says that God has good works "prepared in advance for us to do." Have you ever thought about the fact that as you go through your day, God has already planned out good works he'd like for you to do? How might having that mind-set change the way you live?
7. The passage says that we are God's "workmanship." The word translated *workmanship* can also be translated as *poetry*. The idea is that God is an artist who wants to make something beautiful out of our lives.

How do you think really accepting God's love into our lives and then giving it away in acts of guerrilla love could make our lives into something beautiful?

8. What do you think God might be trying to say to you through this chapter and these questions? What will you do about it?

It's Time to Get Guerrilla

From here on out the chapters will end not only with questions but also with a challenge to apply what you have read. Ingesting the ideas in this book is not enough; you need to use them, to live them out. It's time to get guerrilla.

Our goal is to become guerrilla lovers. That should become our identity and the normal way we live life. But sometimes we need help getting started with something new to us. I gave my church mandatory guerrilla lover assignments to get people started. Here are a few for you. Choose one and do it in the next 48 hours.

1. Bring in something special for your kid's teacher.
2. Write a thank-you note to someone who has influenced your life.
3. Serve hot coffee in front of an office building in the morning as people come in for work.
4. Bring a $20 tip to the kitchen of a restaurant and give it to the dishwasher.
5. Give a plate of cookies to a city worker (garbage collector, police officer, firefighter, or postal worker).
6. Mow your neighbor's lawn or wash their car.
7. Send a care package to someone in the military, a college student, or someone in prison who you know and suspect doesn't receive care packages.
8. Go to a restaurant and pay for someone else's meal.

9

GUERRILLA MERCY-NARIES

You really need to understand how hard it was raining. That's my excuse. It's why I hit the car, why I ended up looking like Mary Poppins, all of it. It's because it was raining. Hard.

We had needed a new CD player for a while, and a store was having a huge sale. So my wife and I bundled up our six-month-old son, ran out to our brand new minivan, and drove to the store. We ran through the rain to the store, picked out the stereo, and paid for it. I told my wife to get our son bundled back up and I would bring the car around to the entrance. I got the car and pulled it around, and my wife brought our son out to the car.

We now had to drive over to the pick-up spot. It was down a slight hill, and the quickest way was to back down it, so I looked back and put the car in reverse. As we reached the bottom of the hill, we suddenly heard a loud, metallic crunch.

I assumed I had run into a pole, but when I opened my door and looked back, I realized that I had hit a car. A brand-new, white Mercedes-Benz. I sighed, grabbed an umbrella, and walked back to see the damage. I found that our back door had a large dent in it but there was absolutely no damage to the other car. I walked back to the driver's side door to tell my wife the news.

I noticed the owner of the car leaving the store and approaching me. He was still a long way off, but I noticed that he looked a lot like the rap singer Snoop Dogg. I shouted from under my umbrella, "Hey!"

He yelled back, "You f-ing, p-ing, q-ing . . ." I noticed he was very creative with his profanity.

"You don't understand," I explained. "There's no damage to your car at all."

He screamed, "I'm gonna break your h-ing, d-ing, s-ing . . ."

"No," I said. "Your car is fine."

He was now inches from me, and he reared back and took a huge swing at me, but *missed*.

"Dude!" I shouted.

He pulled back and swung with all his might, aiming for my head, but *missed again*.

"Calm down, man!"

He was getting angrier by the second. He drew back and threw his fist at my face, and I felt it whiz past my ear.

Before I tell you what happened next, I'll share with you my three theories for why all of his punches missed without my even ducking: (1) The man lacked depth perception. Maybe he wasn't wearing his glasses, or maybe he always lived with this disability. (2) God was protecting me. Now this is the most spiritual answer, and has been suggested by several of my friends who have heard this story, but it's not my best guess. No, personally I think (3) it was the umbrella. Remember, as Snoop Dogg was swinging at me, I was standing there looking like Mary Poppins. The only way I could have been more Mary Poppins–like was if I had been singing, "A spoonful of sugar makes the medicine go down" in between punches. I believe that the umbrella was what threw off the man's aim. And I thank God to this day for that umbrella.

So here's what happened next.

My typically mild-mannered wife rolled down the driver's side window and *screamed*, "What are you doing? People don't do this! You are hitting a minister!"

I would do *anything* to have that moment on video. I would replay it over and over again, peeing my pants in hilarious delight.

Then my wife stormed out her door, came around the front of the minivan, and screamed at Snoop Dogg, "I'm calling the cops!"

I stopped her and said, "No, you're not."

"Let's get out of here!" Snoop Dogg's friend was yelling to Snoop Dogg.

"Why not?" my wife was yelling at me.

"Because of Jesus," I said.

"What does Jesus have to do with this?" my wife asked.

"Remember," I answered, "'If someone strikes you on the right cheek, turn to him the other also' and 'Love your enemies'? We don't get to pick and choose when we obey those. We're supposed to be different. We show mercy."

I turned around and yelled over to Snoop Dogg, "Let's exchange insurance information."

He yelled back, "No way! You r-ing, f-ing, d-ing . . . I'm out of here!" He jumped in his car and took off.

"Forshizzle?" I called out as he drove away. "What about our insurizzle informizzle?" (Okay, I didn't really say that, but the only thing that held me back is that it just felt wrong, with me looking all Mary Poppins at the time.)

♥

Jesus came to unleash a worldwide revolution of love, and the revolution is spread through forgiveness.[1] We are to love people into the movement. We are to grace people into the movement. We are to forgive people into the movement. We are guerrilla mercy-naries.

A woman named Colette attends my church. When she first showed up she was new to all this "God stuff," but she quickly embraced Jesus and joined his revolution.

Then the unthinkable happened: her husband left her. Adding insult to injury, he left her for one of her best friends. It was too much to bear. Her first emotions were anger and hatred, her first thoughts of revenge.

But as she prayed about what was happening to her and processed it with some of her new Christian friends, she slowly started seeing it in a different way. She began seeing it through the eyes of Jesus, the one who looked down from his cross and prayed, "Father, forgive them," for those who had nailed him there.

One Sunday morning she was thinking and praying about this, when suddenly she realized what she had to do. She picked up her phone and called her former best friend, who was now with her husband. When the woman realized it was Colette, she became very anxious until she finally understood why Colette was calling. Colette made an extraordinary invitation. She asked her husband's mistress if she would please come to church with Colette. The woman paused, startled, but then said yes. That morning they walked into church and sat together, and Colette's friend learned of the one who can forgive anyone any sin and whose forgiveness can turn a life around.

A twelve-year-old named Jacob has been coming to our church most of his young life. One chilly November morning Jacob left his house to walk to the bus stop. As he walked up something stopped him—a rock. The kids at the bus stop were throwing rocks at him. They were also shouting, "You're fat." "Go home!" "Don't cry, you fat f—!" Jacob ran home, blinded with rage and shame, tasting the salt of his tears. His mother was surprised to see him, but after learning what had happened, she told Jacob she would drive him to school.

Jacob knew the same bullies would be at school and begged to stay home, but his mother insisted he go.

That night the rest of his family heard about what had happened. His older brother said, "Tomorrow morning we're gonna go there together and beat those kids up." His parents discussed calling the bullies' parents.

But by this point Jacob had a different idea.

He explained he wanted to invite the kid who had been most abusive to sleep over on Saturday night and go with the family to church on Sunday. His parents were flabbergasted. They asked, "Jacob, why would you want to do that? I mean, after what he did to you?"

Jacob explained that in youth group the week earlier he had learned about *grace*. He had been taught that grace means to get the opposite of what you deserve. Grace is how God treats us and how he asks us to treat others. Jacob said he wanted to show that bully God's grace.

The next day Jacob invited his attacker to sleep over and come to church with his family. Surprisingly, the boy said yes. That Saturday night he slept over, that Sunday he came to church, and he's been going to church with Jacob every Sunday since.

Last year my eight-year-old son Dawson came home from school very upset. A boy in his class named Dre had stolen two of his pencils, denied doing it, and then broke one of the pencils right in front of Dawson's face. My son told me he was not going to school the next day. He didn't want to deal with this bully and was afraid of what Dre might do. I said, "Dawson, you know what we're going to do to him? We're going to kill him." This surprised Dawson, but he seemed rather pleased by the idea. I continued, "We're going to kill him . . . with kindness."

"Kill him with kindness?" Dawson asked. His enthusiasm was waning.

"Yes, we're going to kill him with kindness. The best thing to do with an enemy is make him your friend. And remember, you represent God in that school. You're a guerrilla lover. So we're going to kill Dre with kindness."

"With kindness?" Dawson was now clearly disappointed. "Dad, I don't really understand what you mean."

I told Dawson the story of Jacob and how he had invited the bully to sleep over and go to church. Dawson started to get a little more excited about the idea. We began plotting how we could kill Dre with kindness.

The next day Dawson walked right up to Dre and said, "I know you stole my pencils yesterday. So I thought maybe you needed some more." Dawson handed him four brand-new pencils. "Here you go."

Dre was shocked. He stared at Dawson cautiously, then, finally accepting that this wasn't a trick, a broad smile spread across his face. "Wow. Thanks, Dawson!"

Dre and Dawson have been friends ever since.

Maybe a question you're asking is: how does someone become a guerrilla mercy-nary? Forgiving is not easy, so how do people like Collette and Jacob and Dawson do it?

I think the answer is that you can't give away something you don't have. People who give forgiveness are people who have received forgiveness.

When Dawson and my daughter Marissa were young, I desperately wanted to help them understand God's offer of forgiveness and that Jesus had to suffer so we could be forgiven. So I came up with a crazy idea. I sat the kids down and shared with them that from now on, if one of them did something wrong and deserved a spanking, the other (the innocent child) could elect to take the spanking. I explained that this is what Jesus did for us. We were guilty, he was innocent, but he chose to "take our spanking." (Substitutionary atonement for toddlers!)

They seemed to understand, but no one got in trouble for a long time, so we didn't have a chance to test out my new system.

One day almost a year later we were driving somewhere and the kids were acting up, especially Marissa, and I gave them a warning or two. Then I realized it might be a good chance to remind them of our family's spanking policy. I explained that if Marissa kept up her bad behavior and it warranted a spanking, Dawson could choose to take the spanking for her. It got quiet in the car for a couple minutes, and then Marissa started whining. I asked why and she said, "Daddyyyyy, when do I get to spank Dawson? I want to spank Dawson!"

Isn't that funny? Marissa was given a chance to avoid a punishment she deserved, and instead of being grateful, all she wanted was to dole out punishment on someone else. The problem with Marissa was that she wasn't viewing herself as being guilty and in need of mercy, but instead she put herself in the role of judge.

That's our problem too. The reason we find forgiving so difficult is because we play judge, and so we're quick to determine guilt and assign penalties, rather than viewing ourselves as in need of mercy. And that makes all the difference.

Did you read the story about Mark Morice? Shortly after Hurricane Katrina hit, Mark Morice saw flood victims hanging on to rooftops and clinging to tree branches. He realized that these people were going to die. He noticed an 18-foot pleasure boat. He didn't know it, but the boat belonged to a man named John Lyons. Mark Morice isn't the kind of guy who steals, but this was a desperate moment that called for desperate measures. Moved by mercy, Morice took the boat and ended up rescuing more than two hundred people with it. Later he passed the boat on to others, who used it to rescue more people. Ultimately the boat was lost. After all the chaos settled down, John Lyons (the boat owner) was looking for the boat, and Mark Morice voluntarily identified himself, explaining that he took the boat and saved all those people in it. John Lyons sued Mark Morice for $12,000.

Why? Because John Lyons put himself in the role of judge rather than viewing himself as someone who needs mercy. If

Mark Morice had saved John Lyons or one of his kids that day, I doubt John Lyons would have filed a lawsuit. Why not? Because he would have seen himself as someone in need of mercy. (I have to admit that when I first heard this story, I wanted to find John Lyons and punch him in the throat. Why? Because I put myself in the role of judge. O irony, thy sting is great.)

If you've been having trouble forgiving, is it because you're viewing yourself as a judge rather than someone in need of mercy? Are you more focused on trying to punish others than on being grateful that you've been forgiven?

The problem is that if we go through life as a judge, unwilling to forgive, we keep ourselves trapped in a cell of our own bitterness. The irony is that we feel like we're making the other person pay by not forgiving them, but we're actually the one suffering. Only when we focus on the fact that we were in need of mercy and received forgiveness are we able to offer forgiveness, releasing and hurling away the past and finally freeing ourselves from the cell of our bitterness.

Wouldn't you like to be a part of a worldwide revolution of love that employs forgiveness as its most powerful weapon?

Then who do you need to forgive?

To whom could you offer an extraordinary invitation?

Who could you kill with kindness?

It's Time to Talk Guerrilla

1. Here's a truth that will seem ridiculously obvious: you can't give something you don't have. It's true, right? You can't give one million dollars if you don't have one million dollars. You can't give a liverwurst sandwich if you don't have a liverwurst sandwich. Agreed? You can't give what you don't have.

2. If you're having a lot of trouble forgiving someone, is it possibly because you don't have forgiveness to give?

Put another way: it's very difficult (or impossible) to give forgiveness if you haven't received forgiveness.

3. Read Colossians 3:12–14. How does this passage connect our receiving God's forgiveness with our ability to give forgiveness to others?

4. How forgiven by God do you feel—not just in your brain but in your heart? Have you ever accepted his forgiveness, and if so, have you really let it sink into your heart so that you *feel* forgiven?

5. Read Matthew 18:21–35. In this story Jesus connects being forgiven with giving forgiveness. Why do you think the man who was forgiven his debt wasn't able to forgive the debt of his fellow servant?

6. Do you think it's possible that this servant didn't *feel* forgiven? Perhaps he still felt like he had to pay back the debt (even though he didn't), or maybe the idea of his debt being forgiven was still so new, he hadn't accepted it yet. What do you think—is it possible he didn't feel forgiven? Why or why not?

7. How can not feeling forgiven make offering forgiveness difficult?

8. If you don't totally feel forgiven by God, how could you get to a place where you do feel that way?

9. Who are you having trouble forgiving?

10. How might it advance the revolution for you to forgive that person?

It's Time to Get Guerrilla

You have a three-part mission (should you decide to accept it) (cue music now):

1. Read "It's Time to Talk Guerrilla." If you realize that you don't *feel* forgiven, get alone with God and beg

him to help you really let his forgiveness flood into your heart. This has to come first.

2. Now it's time to offer forgiveness. Benedictine monks have a daily practice to remind them that they need God's grace to offer forgiveness to others. They get a bucket of water. Then they identify (in their mind) a person they have not forgiven, and they symbolically hold that person in their clenched fists and put their fists into the water. They then pray for the grace to forgive that person. As they feel God working his grace into their heart, they gradually open their fists, symbolically releasing the grudge they've held. So go fill a bucket with water and get all Benedictine. This may take serious prayer and a decent amount of time, so give yourself a while.

3. Now you're going to leave behind Benedictine and go guerrilla. Pray about what would be the most appropriate way to let that person know you have forgiven him or her. Not the *easiest* way but the *most appropriate* way. Usually this will be in a face-to-face meeting. In some situations, meeting with the person may not be appropriate (for instance, with a person who may pose some physical danger to you). Whatever is most appropriate (meet face-to-face, make a phone call, write a letter), do it. Let that person know that you have forgiven him or her and that it's because God has forgiven you.

You know how shampoo bottles always say, "Lather, rinse, repeat"? Well, Benedictine monks repeat this process *every day*. It may be a good idea for you to do it at least once a month. Maybe you should go to whatever calendar you use and mark a day each month (perhaps the first Sunday of every month) when you will create some time to engage in this process.

For more assignments and ideas, and to learn about and become a part of the Guerrilla Lover movement, go to www .guerrillalovers.com.

10

FREEDOM FIGHTERS

Can you remember a time when you felt stuck? Trapped? Locked up behind a wall with seemingly no means of escape?

Perhaps it was a suffocating marriage.

An addiction that had its claws in you and would not let go.

An avalanche of debt that was crushing you under its weight.

A depression that hovered over you like an ever-present fog.

An abusive relationship.

And all you wanted was to get unstuck. To get untrapped. To get . . . free.

♥

On a Sunday morning not too long ago, about a half hour before our church service was to begin, I made my way into the men's restroom. I typically will make sure all the liquid has been removed from my system before I go up to preach, but this time was different. You understand. So I entered the stall. Soon I was done with business, but there was a problem. I couldn't leave. The door to the stall would not open. I unlocked it. I turned the handle one way and then the other. I pulled. I pushed. I slammed my body against the door. But it would not open. I seriously could not get out.

It was time to evaluate my options. One, I could crawl under the door. The idea of sliding my body along a men's bathroom floor did not hold a lot of appeal, but for a moment it seemed the best escape plan. That was, until I examined the space under the door. There was no way my body would fit through it.

Two, I could just remain in the stall and skip the church service. This was the most attractive alternative, except for a few glaring weaknesses, like that our service would have a conspicuous lack of a pastor and sermon. And at some point there would come a time when I would have to leave the stall. I also wasn't sure about how the odor involved in hanging out in the bathroom for an extended period of time would impact me.

Three, I could start screaming for help. This would probably lead to my liberation from captivity, but the thought of some guy saving me from a bathroom stall brought upon me an unholy terror.

I was stuck.[1]

That experience left me with a low-grade shame and a resolution that I would never speak of it, until just recently when my wife cut an article out of the newspaper for me. You're not going to believe this one, and I wish it wasn't true, but it is. I won't build up to it, I'll just open with the article's title: "Woman Stays on Toilet for Two Years."[2]

Yeah, I told you.

It seems a thirty-five-year-old woman in Ness City, Kansas, sat on her boyfriend's toilet . . . *for two years*! By the time her boyfriend finally called the police for help, her body was stuck to the seat. Ness County Sheriff Bryan Whipple explained, "She was not glued. She was not tied. She was just physically stuck by her body." He said it appeared that her skin had grown around the seat.

Apparently each day her boyfriend had brought her food and water and asked her to come out of the bathroom. Her reply? "Maybe tomorrow." Finally, on February 27, 2008, the boyfriend decided that two years on the toilet was enough. Police reported that the clothed woman was sitting on the toilet with her sweatpants down to her mid-thigh, that she was "somewhat disoriented," and that her legs looked like they had atrophied. Amazingly, a neighbor named James Ellis said, upon hearing of the situation, "It really doesn't surprise me." What kind of neighborhood do these people live in?

I honestly didn't know how to respond to that story. I had to read it again. I thought, "There's no way this could be true." And, "But how? Why? Why didn't the woman just get up? Call for help? Do something?"

I look back at times in my life when I've felt stuck, and from my current vantage point, I can hardly believe I stayed in the situation for so long. Yet I can clearly recall that feeling of helplessness.

Did you know that *most* people feel that way? People you know, live next to, work with, see every day—they don't show it or admit it, but they feel stuck, trapped, locked up behind a wall with no apparent means of escape. And what they desperately want, and need, is freedom.

We could debate about how the situation they're in is their fault because of bad decisions they've made along the way. And, yes, there's probably some truth in that. But still, it's not like this is what they wanted. No one ever grew up thinking, "When I get older, I want to be a child molester." No one ever wrote on a piece of paper, "My life goal is to be an addict," or "Someday I hope to become an alcoholic." People who are addicted to pornography aren't proud of it. No, they think, "Look at me. I'm a forty-year-old man staring at images of naked young girls on a computer screen. What's wrong with me?" Wives who have been unfaithful to their husbands didn't go into their marriage hoping to destroy it. They don't want to set that example for their kids. They don't want to be known as an adulteress. Husbands who beat their wives don't take joy in it. High school girls who are sleeping around didn't dream, growing up, of being called a whore. Parents don't want to have a lack of patience and scream at their kids all the time.

What all these people want—desperately want—and need is freedom.

The Berlin wall fell on November 9, 1989. In his memoir *The Politics of Diplomacy*, James Baker recalls visiting the now punctured and broken wall in December 1990. "As I peered through a crack in the Wall . . . and saw the high-resolution drabness that characterizes East Berlin, I realized that the ordinary men and women of East Germany, peacefully and persistently, had taken matters into their own hands. This was their revolution."[3]

I love that. I love the idea of peeking through a small crack in a wall that had for so long kept people in bondage and catching a glimpse of freedom.

Interestingly, the revolution seems to have been fueled by something more powerful than persistence. In the late 1970s East German churches began uniting in prayer. By 1989 prayer rallies in the city of Leipzig were attracting 300,000 people. Similar events brought together a million or more in Berlin. The state began preparing for a violent rebellion, putting snipers on church roofs and tanks on the streets. When the wall finally came down, one Communist official made an extraordinary admission to a journalist: "We were prepared for every eventuality, but not for candles and not for prayers."[4]

The people of East Germany gained freedom from the bondage of Communism (at least in part) because of the power of God unleashed through their prayers.

But your friends, neighbors, and coworkers who are stuck (in the bathroom stall or on the toilet of life) but don't know God will *not* pray. They may dream of freedom, they may even peek at it through cracks in the wall, but they have no idea how to get there.

So how will they get there? Who will pray for them? Who will fight and persist and point the way for them?

You will.

Some hold a stereotype that God is mean in the Old Testament and nice in the New Testament. That is not the case. We see God giving grace throughout the entire Bible. But it is true that we sometimes see God get angry in the Old Testament. On one particular occasion, we see God taking his people to the woodshed. For what, you ask?

> Therefore, this is what the LORD says: You have not obeyed me; *you have not proclaimed freedom for your fellow countrymen.* So I now proclaim "freedom" for you, declares the LORD—"freedom" to fall by the sword, plague and famine. I will make you abhorrent to all the kingdoms of the earth.[5]

God tells us we can hardly think we're living in obedience to him if we're not proclaiming freedom to others.

Then, in the New Testament, Jesus comes along, and in his first recorded sermon he declares why his Father had him come to earth: "He has sent me to proclaim freedom."[6] And all those who follow in the way of Jesus walk this same path. We are to proclaim freedom.

Because this is what guerrilla lovers do.

We are freedom fighters.

When I think of freedom fighters, I think of my wife, Jennifer. Jennifer knows what it feels like to live in bondage. As a young teenager she started suffering with major depression. It was nearly uninterrupted, unexplainable, massive depression. I met her when she was twenty. Things had gotten so bad that whenever possible she would not get out of bed, trying to sleep her life away rather than experience it.

Now, sixteen years later, not only is Jen free from depression, she has played a significant role in freeing many other women from it as well. So how did she go from being confined behind a seemingly impenetrable wall of despair to helping other women peek through and then break through the walls that held them in?

First, she focused intensely on herself. Now, most everyone I know is focused on themselves, and I think that may be our biggest problem, and it's the reason I'm writing this book. But Jen focused on herself in a very different way.

Most people are agents for their own happiness. They do what leads to their feeling good. Jen took a very different approach. She became dedicated not to her happiness but to her wholeness. Instead of doing what made her feel good, she began doing what would lead to her being healthy. In fact, most of the actions she took made her feel *bad*. She sat through hours of painful counseling. She read books that made her feel uncomfortable. She asked people to keep her accountable.

She had spent twenty years digging down into a pit of depression, so getting out of it was not going to happen overnight.

It took years.

But Jen, though discouraged at times, never gave up. She continued to focus intensely on herself, on her wholeness, on her holiness. She did whatever it took. When she fell down, she got back up and kept walking.

What about you? Are you focusing intensely on yourself? Not on your happiness but on your wholeness. Not on what makes you feel good but on what makes you healthy.

Most of us live with this delusion that if I do what I want to do now, I will still become a person worth becoming.

You won't.

What we want to do in this moment is rarely what's best for us. We need to take a longer view of life and to realize that to become someone worth becoming, I probably need to be doing things I don't want to be doing.

What might that mean for you?

Instead of watching TV tonight, maybe you need to attend that meeting.

Instead of writing another email that glosses over the problems, maybe you need to show up at her house.

Instead of continuing to assume that seminar wouldn't work for you like it's worked for them, maybe you need to sign up and take it.

Instead of hoping it won't happen again, maybe you need to confess your sin so you have a friend making sure it doesn't happen again.

To become a freedom fighter, you must be free. Again, you can't give away something you don't have. So first you need to fight for your own freedom.

Second, Jen focused intensely on other people. One of my favorite people from American history is Harriet Tubman. She was born into slavery and lived in it until 1849 when she took her emancipation into her own hands, escaping north to Philadelphia from a plantation in Maryland. The first thing she did once she escaped was . . . go back. She returned to Maryland to free her sister and her sister's family. She returned again to free three of her brothers. Then again to free her parents. She ended up returning on eighteen or nineteen rescue missions, bringing a total of over two hundred people out of slavery.

That totally makes her a hero. And in one sense I think it's amazing that once free, she didn't decide to just play it safe and enjoy her freedom.

But in another sense I think, how could she *not* return? I mean, if you've spent your life in the horrors of slavery and you know that people are still trapped in it, don't you *have* to go back?

As soon as Jen began finding freedom from her depression, she started focusing intensely on other people. Every time she heard about some woman who was struggling with hopelessness, she would go back. She returned to teach classes for women in our church on how to find freedom from despair. When she was asked to speak to pastors' wives at conferences, she shared her story of slavery to depression and showed them the path to emancipation.

It certainly would have been easier for Jen to just enjoy her freedom. It's never fun to enter into the darkness of another person's depression. Having to repeatedly go back and relive painful memories is, well, painful. But Jen chose to focus intensely on other people.

Have you made that choice? Maybe you've gotten through something and when you did you thought, *I am leaving that behind and will never return.* And that's a great way of thinking . . . for selfish jerks.

If we actually care about people other than ourselves, we *can't* leave our problems behind and never return. If we don't take the freedom we've experienced and try to bring it to others, we are *not* becoming people worth becoming. What we're becoming is the center of a very small universe that is not worth living in because we have to live with ourselves in it. If that's where you've been living, it is imperative that you get the heck out of Dodge. And if you're leaving and wondering where you should go, go back. Return to the people who are struggling with problems you've gone through, people in pain you can relate to, people wrestling with issues you've dealt with.

The reason we need to do this is simple yet profound. It has nothing to do with our happiness and everything to do with our wholeness. Really, it's about who we are: freedom fighters.

Several years ago the city of Philadelphia began passing anti-homeless legislation. They made it illegal to sleep in parks, ask for money, or lie down on the sidewalks. Part of the impetus for these laws was Love Park, a historic site in Philly and a place where the homeless chose to congregate. People who cared about the plight of the homeless knew they could go there to give out food. To stop this, the city passed an ordinance banning the distribution of food in parks.

When this all went down, a group of Christian students from a nearby college heard about it. These students had in the past often visited Love Park to hang out with the homeless and give them food, in hopes of showing them the love of God.

When they heard about the new legislation, they debated amongst themselves what to do. How could they continue to show love to the homeless? Should they obey these laws? Or should they follow the wisdom of Saint Augustine, who said, "An unjust law is no law at all"?

They decided, as an act of solidarity with their homeless friends, to throw a party at Love Park. About a hundred of them gathered in Love Park with the homeless. They worshiped, sang, and prayed. They served communion, which was illegal.

Police surrounded the park but did nothing, probably because they were afraid of the bad press it would get them. Can you picture the headlines? "College Students Brought to the Slammer in Handcuffs . . . for Taking Communion in Park!"

The Christian students saw that they weren't getting arrested and their homeless friends were still hungry (communion is great for spiritual sustenance but is not always especially filling), so they ordered pizzas.

When the party was over, the kids from the college realized that if the homeless stayed, they would get arrested for sleeping in the park, so the students stayed overnight in the park. And this continued day after day, night after night, week after week, with the police and media watching it all.

Finally the police had enough and arrested all of them. The story received so much media attention that a bunch of bigwig attorneys called, offering to represent the students. But they politely refused, instead deciding to be represented by a homeless man named Fonz.

Finally the day came for their trial. The students stood before the judge, one of them wearing a "Jesus was homeless" T-shirt.

The judge asked him to step forward, read the shirt aloud, and said, "Hmm. I didn't know that."

The student replied, "Yes sir, in the Scriptures Jesus says that 'foxes have holes and birds have nests but the Son of Man has no place to lay his head.'"

The judge paused and said, "You guys might stand a chance."

When the time came for their defense, Fonz stood up and said, "Your honor, we think these laws are wrong."

And the big group of Christians and homeless people in the courtroom shouted, "Amen. What he said!"

Then the district attorney made her case, asking for jail time and thousands of dollars in fines. The judge said to the court, "What is in question here is not whether these folks broke the law; that is quite clear. What is in question is the constitutionality of the law."

The D.A. shot back, "The constitutionality of the law is not before this court."

The judge retorted, "The constitutionality of the law is before every court. Let me remind the court that if it weren't for people who broke unjust laws, we wouldn't have the freedom that we have. We'd still have slavery. That's the story of this country, from the Boston Tea Party to the civil rights movement. These people are not criminals; *they are freedom fighters*. I find them not guilty on every charge."

The papers called it a "Revolutionary Court Decision."[7]

And this is our revolution, as guerrilla lovers—we are freedom fighters.

So who could you pray for?

Who could you persist for?

Who could you bust through a wall for?

Who could you sleep in a park for?

Who could you fight for?

Who do you know who is stuck on the toilet of life?

In her book *Leaving Church*, Barbara Brown Taylor describes an experience she had as a pastor at Grace-Calvary Episcopal Church. A grown woman who was allegedly diabetic and her elderly mother would call churches asking for money or groceries. Taylor would usually say yes to their request, but even when she said no, the mother would not take this as discouragement but as a challenge to try harder. One afternoon she called and said, "Martha is sitting on the toilet and we are out of toilet paper. If I came over right now, could you write me a check to the grocery store so she can get up?"[8]

There may be someone you know who is stuck, and all they need is a little bit of toilet paper. Can't you spare a square?

It's what guerrilla lovers do.

We proclaim freedom.

We are freedom fighters.

It's Time to Talk Guerrilla

1. Read Luke 4:16–21. If by quoting the passage from Isaiah, Jesus is in a sense giving his "job description," what surprises you about his job description?

2. What do you think it means that Jesus came to "proclaim freedom for the prisoners"? Do you think it means literal prisoners? Could it include people who are imprisoned by things other than jail cells?

3. In what ways did Jesus accomplish this job description? Did he set prisoners free, and if so, how?
4. If you call yourself a Christian and follow in the way of Jesus, how does his job description apply to you?
5. In what ways are you to proclaim freedom for the prisoners?
6. Can you think of a person you have helped to set free from some kind of bondage?
7. What do you think is the thing that most keeps Christians from being freedom fighters? What do you think has most kept you from fighting for the freedom of others?
8. What could you do to overcome your excuses and take your place in God's revolution as a freedom fighter?

It's Time to Get Guerrilla

Empty your mind. Is it empty? Really? (Wait, maybe that's not so unusual for you.)

Okay, now it's time to fill your mind, and you're going to fill it with a person (or a group of people). Think about a person you know who is in prison. A person who is stuck in some situation, relationship, or addiction.

Now empty your mind again. Ready? Ask God what you could do to help that person get "unstuck." Do it. Now.

What did he tell you? If he told you something . . . do it. If you don't feel like you "heard" anything, ask again. Maybe this time, pray this prayer: "God, what is *the most radical thing I could do* to help that person (or group of people) get unstuck?" Go ahead, pray that. Now.

What did he tell you? If you still don't know, keep praying it. If you have an idea but you're not sure if it was God telling you it, just assume it was. Especially assume that if the idea is radical and makes you feel uncomfortable.

Now you might be thinking, "But I don't think I could do that. I'm not sure *how*. I don't know if I have the strength, creativity, speaking ability, intelligence, blah, blah, blah." If that's what you're thinking, that's *perfect*, because God *does have* the strength, creativity, speaking ability, intelligence, and so on. And God loves to work through our weakness, because it forces us to rely on him and because that way he gets the glory.

So are you ready to get guerrilla? Go "unstuck" somebody!

For more assignments and ideas, and to learn about and become a part of the Guerrilla Lover movement, go to www .guerrillalovers.com.

KINGDOM PARTIES

Pop quiz! Who said the following: "Party, or I will kill you"? Was it (a) Hugh Hefner, (b) the Beastie Boys, (c) Paris Hilton, or (d) God?

You can find the answer in Leviticus 23.

In addition to being a long and sometimes dreary book, Leviticus records God planning out parties for his people. He apparently takes these parties very seriously since the death sentence is the penalty for avoiding them.

Lest we think that perhaps God was not himself when he was playing party planner back in Leviticus, we also have the example of Jesus. Jesus was known to show up at a party or two. In fact, Jesus was called a glutton and a drunkard—not because he was but because he hung out so much with gluttons and drunkards. It was guilt by association.

Jesus loved a good party.

In fact, pop quiz #2: What was Jesus's first miracle? Was it: (a) raising a widow's dead son, (b) healing a man born blind,

(c) revitalizing the career of John Travolta, or (d) turning 120 gallons of water into wine for a party.

You can find the answer in John 2.

By any standard 120 gallons is a lot of wine. I have no interest in causing a theological debate about drinking alcohol, so I will simply provide a straightforward reporting of the facts: There was a party. Jesus went to the party. The wine ran out. The host feared the guests would become disgruntled, perhaps even leave, so Jesus turned 120 gallons of water into wine. The party continued, and people sang, "Tonight we're gonna party like it's 0-0-99!" (That last bit is just a rumor. I cannot confirm it.)

Jesus regularly attended parties, and he also spoke of them. In fact, partying is a centerpiece in Jesus's teaching. He repeatedly compared his kingdom and heaven to a party.[1]

So, pop quiz #3: How is it that Christians have become known as the anti-partiers? When we worship a God who demands partying and follow a Savior who seems to have beaten Spuds MacKenzie to the punch in being "the original party animal" and "the guru of good times"—how is it that we have become the anti-partiers?

Answer: I have no idea.

I am not endorsing drunken rages, orgies, or even spin the bottle.

But I am saying that we should be party throwers.

And I am wondering if part of the reason we have such a bad reputation is because we have been party poopers.

My church, Forefront, has always focused on reaching out to those who seem the farthest from God and the least interested in church. That mission led us to wonder about the Sunday morning services we were holding in high school auditoriums. This was working for many people. But was it possible that some were not being reached in part because we met on Sunday mornings in a high school?

Sunday mornings have been effective for churches for thousands of years, but was it the best time for everyone today? We asked around, and a variety of people told us it was not. Some explained that it was their "sleep in" morning, others told us it was their beach day or kids' soccer tournament time, but mostly we heard from people that Sunday mornings were not ideal because they were hung over from the night before.

These were not Christians, of course. Christians have powerful motivations for going to church, but non-Christians don't think they should go to church. So why go if there's *any* reason not to? Hey, I don't eat Afghani food. I'm not going to eat Afghani food just because a restaurant is open on Sunday mornings. And if I was open to trying it and was invited to do so, but the restaurant was *only* open on Sunday mornings and I had something else going on at that time, well, no thanks.

We also realized that though a school was neutral territory (and therefore better than a church building), it was not exactly attractive. Very few people upon graduating from high school think, "I hope someday I have a reason to go back there." There are certainly worse places to have a church service (a morgue, DMV, or dentist's office), but a school wasn't ideal.

This process ultimately led us to open a third "campus" of our church with a service that met on *Tuesday nights* in a *bar* called the White Horse Pub.[2] The bar would be open for business, serving food and alcohol, while we conducted our service.

The owner was willing to have us in part because he is a rebel and, while most would say it's "religious" to let a church meet in a bar, he considers it rebellious. He's "sticking it to the man"—though I haven't figured out what he's sticking, where he's sticking it, or who exactly the man is.

The other reason he was down with the idea is business. We quickly packed the place out. He added more waitresses and an extra bartender.

We had a "practice service," but it wasn't much of a "practice" since the bar was open for business and about twenty guys were there drinking. They were very surprised to find worship music and a sermon and communion happening all around them. After the service someone asked them what they thought of a church meeting in their bar and of our service itself. One guy said, "It's been a long time comin'!" Another jumped in, "The sermon made me laugh my a— off." Someone else added, "You guys know how to make church fun." And another, "I could do *this* church."

When we arrived to set up at 4:00 in the afternoon the following Tuesday for our first "real" service, a guy there was, um, shall we say, unsober. He was tanked. Plastered. Schnockered. It was only a matter of time before he'd be cleaning his plumbing out in the parking lot. But for now he decided to hang out with us. He offered to run the sound board, preach the sermon, play the drums. (Well, I can't be sure of that. It sounded more like, "I can bffplaay-urp your uhhh, whatfuba ya ca, lllll, you know, wh-ba, the dawaaa, the dawaaa, the draaaaa, the drumpssthsss.") We kept him away from the sound board and drums and told him he couldn't preach but could do the communion meditation.

Soon the media found out what we were doing, and we had camera crews out on Tuesday nights filming our services for stories on the nightly news. Our local paper also came out and ran a front page story, which was then picked up by newspapers around the country. That was cool, except that I was described in the article as "A husky 30-something with an urgent air."[3] That is so *un*cool. Why not just say, "Vince is a fat, neurotic 30-something," or "Small children run in fear from Vince because of his gargantuan size and insane demeanor"?

The paper had an online version of the story featured on their website, on which people could leave comments. Immediately the comments section spilled into multiple pages as Christians duked it out publicly over whether it was appropriate for a church to meet in a bar or for Christians to even be around alcohol. While many Christians cheered and defended the idea of having a service in the bar as a way of reaching out to people who would not feel comfortable coming to a church building, others attacked us.

William W. of Norfolk commented: "I don't believe that a bar is the proper setting for a church service. There is smoking, drinking, and foul language at these places."

Steve L. of Virginia Beach wrote, "This is wrong on so many levels. . . . File this under 'Another crackpot religion.'"

Paco F. of Chesapeake said, "People invent their own religions all the time. . . . They will sacrifice everything for it (Jim Jones comes to mind). . . . The true church is a gathering of believers. 'Forefront Church' is not a church."

And then the non-Christians started responding. This is where it got depressingly sad.

Amy C. of Chesapeake commented, "Just reading these comments makes me remember why you will not get me in a church on a Sunday."

Paul M. of Norfolk wrote, "I can't help but find humor in the fact that all the Christians here can't seem to agree on anything! . . . All religion does is cause dissension between people who might otherwise get along."

Jeffery M. of Virginia Beach asked, "Perhaps you are more comfortable with the 5,000 seat arena with cappuccino bars? Heaven forbid an ex-con should sit down next to you in the pews?"

Louise G. of Norfolk commented, "I find the entire ritual of attending church, regardless of where it is held, disheartening."

And Peter C. of Norfolk wrote, "After reading some of these comments . . . I think I need a drink."

Christians are certainly entitled to their own views on alcohol and the proper facilities in which to have church services. I will not fault anyone for their opinions. But there is a right way to state your opinions. And the comments left by Christians just further turned people off to Christianity and continued to establish their reputation as holier-than-thou anti-partiers—exactly the opposite of what Jesus was known for.

Meanwhile, as the controversy continued to fume, we chose not to defend ourselves but instead to just keep doing services on Tuesday nights in the bar.

I thought of myself as someone who knows Christians should be party-throwers, but I quickly discovered that I didn't understand that concept as well as others did.

After our first service a guy walked up to me and said, "Hey, man." I turned around and saw that he was bigger than me. Having someone yell a curse word at me during the sermon had put me on high alert, so I assumed he was going to beat me up. I started considering my options: (1) scream like a little girl, (2) tell him I'm a pacifist, (3) kick him in the groin, or (4) run, but I quickly decided on option (5): scream like a little girl, *then* tell him I'm a pacifist, *then* kick him in the groin (he won't be expecting it after the pacifist remark), *then* run.

That's when I looked up and saw tears in his eyes. My first thought was, "Hey, maybe I *can* take him. He's a wimp!" My second was, "Why is he crying?"

He gulped and said, "Yeah, um, well, thanks for teaching me about forgiveness," and then he quickly walked away, like he was embarrassed.

The next week he was back. After the service I approached him and said, "Hey, thanks for coming back."

"No, thank *you*," he responded. "I would *never* go to church on a Sunday morning. This is perfect for me. Thank you for doing this for me."

"Of course," I answered. "We're just glad to be here."
Then he said, "Can I ask you a question? How much would
it cost me for a service?"

I was confused. "Sorry, what do you mean?"

"How much would it cost me to get a service?" he asked
again.

I groped for what he might be referring to. "Do you mean
our band?"

"Yeah," he answered.

"Ohhhh." I felt relieved. "Yeah, they play at all kinds of
stuff. I don't know how much it would cost. You'd have to
ask Joe."

"Okay," he started, "well, let me tell you my idea. See, I
have a huge backyard, *huge*, and I throw huge parties. *Huge!*
So I'll invite all my friends. And I'll buy all the food and all
the drinks, and I'd like to have a service."

I was confused again. "A service?"

"Yeah," he was excited now. "I'm going to invite all my
friends, and then surprise them with a service. Just like what
you guys did tonight. I want the band, the sermon, the videos,
communion."

"Wait a second," I said. "You mean you want to have a
church service in your backyard for your friends?"

"Yeah! Just like what you did tonight. It will be a great
party. So how much do I have to pay for that?"

"Dude," I was smiling now, "if you invite all your friends
over and let us have a church service in your backyard, you
don't have to pay a thing."

"Really?"

"Really!"

"Wellll, then," he said, searching for an idea. "I'll have you
picked up in a limousine!"

"Uh, no, that's okay. I have a car."

He was surprised. "So you'd come out and do a church
service party for my friends for free?"

"Yes."

"Wow, then you can count on it. We're gonna do it on a Friday night. This will be awesome. It will be a great party and my friends are gonna love this church!"

I walked away feeling like I had just been schooled on being a guerrilla lover. I had this "party theology," but I never would have thought of throwing a "surprise party" for a bunch of non-Christian friends. I should have, because that guy's idea was not original. It's actually biblical. One of Jesus's first followers, a guy named Matthew (or Levi), did just that.[4]

Meanwhile, as this guy dreamed about putting together a party to introduce his friends to God, another party was about to happen. About twenty members of our church had decided to stop attending on Sunday mornings and become the core of our new Tuesday night bar service. One member of that core group is Samantha. We had been talking a lot about being guerrilla lovers, and Samantha felt like being a part of the service at the pub might give her a chance to somehow give people a glimpse of God's love. Because of that, she couldn't help but notice the pregnant bartender, who, it turns out, was an ex-stripper. (Let me make it clear that I have this information secondhand. I *have* seen her wait on tables, but I have *never* seen her strip.) Apparently there's not much call for pregnant strippers, so she had to find a new job, which is why she started bartending at this pub.

But feeling like a guerrilla lover, Samantha couldn't help but notice her. She also couldn't help but start talking to her each week, and she couldn't help but begin praying about how she could ambush this lady with God's love. The answer God gave her was . . .

A party.

She began sharing her idea with some of the other Forefront women, and everyone quickly jumped on board. They had to act fast, because the bartender was only a few weeks away from her due date. They each went shopping and bought a boatload of baby shower presents. Samantha called the bar manager and asked her to call the pregnant bartender in an hour early, pretending it was really busy and they "needed extra help." The manager complied, and the bartender came rushing in . . . to a nearly empty bar, except for the five Forefront women, a table full of presents and food, and a huge "Surprise!" She stopped in her tracks and just stared, not quite able to comprehend what was happening. When she finally got it, she was even more stunned. She couldn't understand why people she didn't know would throw her a party. And not only were these people virtually strangers, they were Christians. Aren't Christians against strippers, against bartenders, against women who get pregnant outside of marriage, and against parties? She was confused, grateful, and pretty much speechless. Samantha says, "I think she had that feeling you get when you don't know God or that he loves you but then you discover for the first time that maybe he does. I think she felt that."

♥

I recently watched the movie *Because of Winn-Dixie*. I wasn't really interested, but Dave Matthews is in it, and my kids wanted to see it. It actually wasn't bad. It's about a young girl named Opal whose mother left her and her father when she was three. She's now about nine years old, and she can't remember her mother and is forced to move from town to town because her father's job as a preacher requires it.

She is lonely. Her father cries over a picture of his wife every day. In yet another new town, Opal meets all kinds of lonely people: an old, blind woman named Gloria who lives by herself in a house deep in the woods; a librarian named Miss Franny with no family; a bitter man named Mr. Alfred who lives in the mobile home next door; and a misunderstood, guitar-playing recluse named Otis. One by one she befriends each of these people, becoming their only friend. And though she feels empty herself, she desperately wants to do something for all her new friends. She says, "I want to help 'em, but I just don't know what to do." Finally she lands on an idea: "We should have a party!"

She talks Gloria into helping her, saying, "Miss Franny said the problem with people here is that they forgot how to share their sadness, but what I think is that people forgot how to share their joy. Gloria, we need this party."

She quickly makes a list of all the lonely people she will invite, but Gloria insists that she also include two neighborhood bullies who have made themselves Opal's enemies. Opal agrees.

Everyone is reluctant to come—they're fearful—but eventually they acquiesce. Soon that old lonely house in the woods is filled with empty people who aren't feeling quite so lonely anymore.

The party starts with Gloria, who was probably the most intimidated by the idea of the party, gathering everyone together to pray. She prays a glorious prayer:

> Dear Lord and heavenly Father: We have egg salad sandwiches, we got Dump's punch, we got pickles, we got doggy pictures, and we have Littmus Lozenges. But more importantly, dear Lord, we have good friends. Dear Lord, we got good friends to share this warm summer night with us, and for that we're grateful. Teach us, dear Lord, to love one another. This we ask in your name. Amen.

Soon someone shouts, "Are we havin' a party, or are we havin' a paaaaarrrrrtttttttyy?"

And Opal says, "My heart doesn't feel so empty anymore. It's full . . . all the way up."

Why? Well, it was because of a party—a party that brought lonely people together and filled all of them up.

As Christians, we need to party.

We need to celebrate.

We need to fill people up.

That's guerrilla love.

It's Time to Talk Guerrilla

1. Before reading this chapter, did you think of God as a pro-partying God? Why or why not?
2. Why do you think God commands his people in the Old Testament to party? Why do you think God's people have lost their passion for celebrating?
3. Read Luke 5:27–31. When Matthew (Levi) meets Jesus, he wants all his friends to meet Jesus as well. Why might Matthew have thought that throwing a party was the best way to accomplish that?
4. Could you throw a party that might help people get a little closer to Jesus?
5. Read Luke 14:12–14. Did you notice that Jesus assumes we'll throw parties? He didn't say, "If you give" a party; he said, "*When* you give" a party. Why do you think he made this assumption?
6. Jesus teaches us that we should use inviting people over as a way of loving people who don't always get loved. Why do you think most Christians don't do what Jesus commands?
7. Jesus compared heaven to a party (see, for instance, Luke 15:7 and 15:22–24). Does that make you more excited about getting to heaven?
8. In what ways do you picture heaven being like a party? In what ways do you think it won't be like a party?
9. Consider spending a night with your group or family watching *Because of Winn-Dixie*. If you do, talk about:
    (a) the acts of guerrilla love you find in the movie and how they help to meet people's needs;
    (b) how each of you could become more like Opal.

It's Time to Get Guerrilla

You are going to throw a party.

Yes, you.

Yes, a party.

And this will not be a lame party. It is going to be a great, fun party that people are glad they came to and talk about for days afterwards. How will you do that? Well, you may pray a lot in advance. And you should probably get some of your friends to help you (your fun friends, not . . . well, you know who). And you'll have music (with a beat) playing. And you'll have games to play. And good food to eat.

You are going to throw a party.

Yes, you.

Yes, a party.

A great party. So you have some decisions to make. Like: Who are you going to ask to help you to throw this party? If you're in a small group or Sunday school class at your church and the people in it have a pulse and know how to laugh, they might work.

And who are you going to invite? If you don't know the people who live in your neighborhood, I would suggest a block party. Another option is a "Matthew party." Invite all the people you know who don't know Jesus and a few of your favorite Christian friends, and see what happens when they get together. You don't have to make any great gospel presentation or take an offering at this party; just let it be fun. Another option is the kind of banquet Jesus mentioned in Luke 14:12–14, where you invite the poor, the crippled, the lame, and the blind. How could you do that? Who could you get to help you? Maybe it could be a church event that you help organize.

"You are going to throw a party . . . or I will kill you." That was a message from God. Now go fight for your right to party!

For more assignments and ideas, and to learn about and become a part of the Guerrilla Lover movement, go to www .guerrillalovers.com.

12

RADICAL HEALERS

One of my favorite T-shirts says, "Love is the movement" on the front.

This is so much better than my old shirt that said on the back, "Uh-oh, just had a bowel movement." (Okay, I never had a shirt that said that. But I wish I did.)

The movement Jesus came to ignite and have revolutionize the world is not about hate, judgment, fear, or intimidation; it's about *love*.

Have you ever wondered how a movement that is supposed to be about love can be so thoroughly despised? It is, by the way. Disdain for the church and for Christianity is widespread these days.

How has this happened for a movement of love?

I think the answer is that we *haven't* been characterized by love.

Instead of loving people, we tend to criticize or ignore them. A small minority of Christians scream into bullhorns on street corners and hold up "God hates fags" signs at protest rallies. The majority of Christians do nothing, living sterile lives from within the confines of their Christian bubble existence, never getting close enough to people's pain to touch it or offer a solution.

People *desperately* need to be loved.

We live in a broken world.

People are hurting.

But the salve for their pain is not medicine or surgery. It's also not the next party, hit, thrill, boyfriend or girlfriend, outfit, cool gadget, or new car. It's love. The unconditional love of God offered through the compassionate concern of a Christian is the only thing that can bring the healing for which people long.

God knew this messed-up world would leave people broken, so he equipped us with what people need: his unconditional love. Hurting people know instinctively they need this, so when we criticize or ignore them instead of loving them, of course they despise us.

The answer is love.

My guess is that if you're reading this book, you probably don't criticize other people all that much.

But if you're anything like me, you do ignore them.

If you're anything like me, you're so preoccupied with yourself that you don't even notice hurting people.

If you're anything like me, you think, "What can *I* possibly do to help?"

♥

The Bible recounts a time when Jesus comes across a funeral procession.[1] A group of people is carrying a dead boy, and they're followed by a crowd of mourners. The dead boy is the only son of his mother, and she is a widow. We don't know much about the situation. How did the widow's husband die? How old was this son? Did the widow have any daughters?

We do know, almost certainly, that the son had died within the last 24 hours. Back then people were buried quickly after death because of the climate and the lack of embalming fluids. So this mother had just lost her son. Probably the shocked numbness was starting to wear off and the rawest moments of pain were starting to set in.

Jesus happens to come across this funeral procession, and the first thing that fascinates me is what Jesus *felt*. We're told, "his heart went out to her."[2] This is translated from the Hebrew word *splagna*. I love that word because it sounds like you retched a few times and then just *spalgnaed* all over the place. And that's actually pretty much what the word means. *Splagna* means to have your guts ripped out. It's that awful feeling you get in your stomach when you see the starving child in Africa covered with flies or the people who just lost their home in a fire. That feeling in your stomach—that's *splagna*. And that's what Jesus felt when he saw this dead boy and this mother who had just lost her only son.

Why does that fascinate me? It was a very ordinary moment; we all have seen a funeral procession before. But Jesus had a very extraordinary reaction. He didn't ignore the scene. He didn't just have a passing sense of pity for the woman. No, he *felt* this mother's pain. His guts were ripped out.

What Jesus feels forces me to ask some hard questions. The last time I went past a hearse, did I even notice? And that socially awkward guy at church, who obviously has some problems—did I avoid him on purpose? When I read the story in the paper about the families who lost their homes to the tornadoes, did it do anything to me? When I drove past the broken-down car, did I even for a second consider stopping to help?

My excuse, if I'm being honest, is that all of that is so normal. I think, *Hearses go by every day . . . If I gave attention to all the socially awkward and needy people, they would consume all my time . . . Tomorrow's paper will tell another story of some family experiencing a tragedy . . . Cars are on the sides of roads everywhere.*

It's all so normal.

That's what's so amazing about Jesus. He had an extraordinary reaction to an ordinary moment. And my problem is that I claim to follow him and I want to live life the way he does, but I often don't.

The second thing that fascinates me is what Jesus *did*. Occasionally I do have an emotional reaction to someone's pain, but even then I typically don't do anything about it. Maybe I don't care enough, or I just feel like there's nothing I can do. Well, Jesus felt something, and then he *did* something.

We're told that he walked up and touched the coffin. I've heard that back then they didn't have coffins like we do, with sides and lids. For them a coffin was just a flat piece of wood on which they would lay the body. And so it may be that Jesus touched the wood, but it's possible Jesus touched the body.

Either way, something startling was happening here. Jesus was crossing some boundaries that people in that day *never* crossed. Back then religion was all about following the rules, about keeping the outward appearance of cleanliness rather than being concerned with actually being pure on the inside. And one of the rules was that you could not touch a dead body. Dead bodies were unclean, and if you touched one, you became unclean. From what I understand, even if Jesus only touched the wood beneath the body, that alone would make him unclean, because that wood had been contaminated by death.

But Jesus's heart went out to this woman, so he ignored the religious policies and touched her dead son. Jesus didn't care about what people thought; he cared about showing compassion.

I imagine that when Jesus touched the boy (or the coffin), the crowd gasped, but then something more shocking happened.

The boy . . . gasped.

Jesus's touch *immediately* brought him back to life.

And, indirectly, it did something just as dramatic for the mother. Back then a widow's only hope was her sons. If you had no husband and no son, you would likely be forced to do horrible things to earn an income. And if this woman had daughters, she would need even more money, or who knows what would have happened to her daughters.

But Jesus touched her son, and he was alive again. We're told that Jesus walked the boy over to his mother. And Jesus not only gave her back her son, he also gave her back her hope.

Again, what Jesus does forces me to ask hard questions. Like, am I willing to touch the sick? Of course my immediate answer is yes, but where's the proof of that? When did I last spend time with someone who truly needed me? When did I last spend time with someone who really made me uncomfortable? And am I willing to break the rules if necessary? What's more important to me: to do things right, or to do the right things? And what about other people? Would I do the right thing if it meant getting a shocked or disappointed look from someone? Am I so into the approval of others that I wouldn't sit down for lunch with a homeless person? Really, I have to ask myself: am I living in such a way that it gives other people hope?

Again, my main problem is Jesus and that I call myself a follower of his. The truth is that I really do want to follow him. I desperately want to live the way he did. But too often I'm able to ignore the needs of others, and even when I do notice, I do nothing about it. I don't take action to bring healing. I don't take my lead from Jesus, who was a radical healer.

♥

That "Love is the movement" shirt I own came from a ministry called To Write Love On Her Arms.[3] In February of 2006 a guy named Jamie Tworkowski met a nineteen-year-old girl named Renee. She had just been denied treatment in a drug rehab center because she had harmed herself by carving words into her arm. Jamie and some of his friends decided to become a support system for her and to offer her the drug rehab the center wouldn't.

They came up with the idea of a five-day rehab. (I think rehabs are typically much longer, but these guys were rookie rehabers.) They decided to make the rehab fun and cool. Jamie wrote about the experience on his MySpace page, and the story, which he called "To Write Love On Her Arms" quickly caught on in his Orlando, Florida, area. Tworkowski and his friends sold T-shirts with the slogan and used the profits to pay for Renee's recovery.

What started out as an attempt to help one girl somehow became a movement. And the movement snowballed. Soon Tworkowski found himself leaving his job to devote all his energy to helping people who suffer from depression, cut themselves, and may be suicidal.

What depresses me to no end is that if I had been the one to come into contact with Renee, I probably wouldn't have noticed her. And if somehow I did, I suspect that I probably would have ignored her. Well, maybe not. Perhaps I would have given her the phone number of a counselor I know. But would I have taken her into my home for five days?

No.

Would I have raised money so I could help her in a way I couldn't afford?

No.

I just wear the T-shirt; I don't start the ministry. I buy the T-shirt to support people who are offering healing to the hurting, but I don't touch the sick myself.

And that's why, sitting here today, I realize that I have a decision to make.

Am I going to be a guerrilla lover or just think that it sounds like a good idea?

And if I'm going to live as a guerrilla lover, what can I do to start noticing hurting people?

And what can I do to start touching their sickness?
I need to notice.
I need to feel pain.
I need to do *something*.
How can I follow in the footsteps of Jesus and become a radical healer?

It's Time to Talk Guerrilla

1. I have a shirt that says, "Love is the movement." If you had to make a shirt promoting Christianity with a slogan on the front that said, "_____ is the movement" and "Love" was not an option, what word would you use?

2. If you had to make a shirt depicting what you believe most non-Christians think about Christianity, how would you fill in the blank: "_____ is the movement"?

3. How have you personally experienced the disdain many outside the faith feel for Christians and the church? What do you think best explains how a movement that is all about love has come to be looked down upon?

4. In the story from Luke 7 shared in this chapter, Jesus felt *splagna*—his heart was broken by problems other people wouldn't even have noticed. What do you think could increase your *splagna*? What changes could you make that would allow you to better feel the pain of others?

5. Jesus not only felt someone's pain, he did something about it. He touched the sick, even though it went against the religious rules of the day. In what ways do you think religious rules and expectations today can keep us from touching the sick?
   (a) What sick person has God put in your life that you could touch?
   (b) How could you touch that person in a way that would give them hope?

6. What are the most common excuses you make for not noticing the pain of others or for not being willing to do something to help them?
7. What inspires you about the story of Jamie Tworkowski and what he and his friends did for Renee, which has now led to an entire ministry?
8. If reading this chapter really led you to take action, what action would you take?

It's Time to Get Guerrilla

In the "Talk Guerrilla" section above, you were asked to think of a sick person you could touch in such a way that you might be able to give him or her a little hope.

It's time to touch.

So who will it be? Here are some categories that may guide your thinking and help you decide on a specific person:

Do you know someone who is physically sick?

Perhaps a person in the hospital?

Or someone with a terminal disease?

Do you know a person who is lonely?

Someone who can't get out of their house?

Someone who has recently been betrayed or dumped?

Do you know someone who is depressed?

Someone who suffers from clinical depression?

Someone who is going through a really difficult time?

Do you know someone who is addicted?

What can you do for this person? What is the action you could take that would show the most compassion (notice the word *passion* in *compassion*—this is not just pity; it's about passion) and bring them the most hope?

Should you visit this person?

Could you bring a meal?

What present might mean the most to him or her?

Or should you write them an encouraging letter?

What words does your friend most need to hear?

Would a phone call be the best option?

Or could you go to a support group with this person?

Have you got it? A person and a way to touch that person? Now go for it.

For more assignments and ideas, and to learn about and become a part of the Guerrilla Lover movement, go to www .guerrillalovers.com.

WOUNDED SOLDIERS

In this chapter I'd like to expose you to two of the eminent classic authors of our time. Yep, that's right, I'm gonna culture y'all just a bit. I did not live in the age of Shakespeare or Dickens, but I do live in the age of these two distinguished authors.

The first . . . Thornton Wilder. One of Wilder's first plays was *The Angel That Troubled the Waters*. The story is based on John 5:1–4, which speaks of a pool in Bethesda where blind, lame, and paralyzed people would wait. Legend had it that an angel would occasionally stir its waters, and the first person in the water after the touch of the angel would be cured of his diseases. Wilder imagines a physician who occasionally would go to the pool, hoping to get in its waters first so he could be healed of his melancholy. Finally the angel appears but blocks the physician just as he is about to enter the water. The angel tells the physician that the healing is not for him. The physician implores the angel to let him in, but to no avail. Finally the angel clarifies why he cannot allow the physician to enter the pool:

> Without your wounds where would your power be? It is your melancholy that makes your low voice tremble into the hearts of men and women. The very angels themselves cannot persuade the wretched and blundering children on earth as can one human being broken on the wheels of living. In Love's service, only wounded soldiers can serve. Physician, draw back.[1]

In the last chapter we talked about being radical healers. How do we become people who don't just wear the T-shirt but actually become a part of God's love movement by touching the sick and bringing healing?

I don't know about you, but that question immediately turns my mind to what strengths I have to offer. I figure, if I'm supposed to help people, well, what do I have to offer them? For instance, I have no plumbing skills, so I will not be able to help in the bathroom.

Are you like me? Does your mind start doing a survey of your strengths, trying to figure out how you can add value to other people's lives?

I wonder if perhaps we need a different way of thinking about this. Wilder introduced the idea, but to develop it further, let's go to the second classic author I want to introduce: Dr. Seuss.

I will admit right up front that I am a big Dr. Seuss fan. I grew up reading his zany stories, and I've used my kids as an excuse to buy and read his books again. I am a fan of the more famous Seuss books like *Green Eggs and Ham* and *The Cat in the Hat*, but perhaps my favorite is the lesser-known *Gerald McBoing Boing*.

Gerald McCloy is a boy who doesn't speak words, only sounds. When he opens his mouth, "Boing! Boing!" comes out. As he gets a little older, his repertoire of sounds increases, but the number of words he can speak remains at zero. Because of this Gerald is expelled from his school and disowned by his parents. He's sent off into the cold, cruel world alone, and he's only in the first grade!

I bet you can relate to Gerald. Not that you *boing-boinged* your way out of the house, but that you have weaknesses and wounds you were born with or have received over the years. We all have them. So what are yours?

And more importantly, what is your attitude toward your weaknesses and wounds? Do you view them the way everyone does: your weaknesses are what make you weak, your wounds are what make you, well, wounded? They are bad things about you, negative attributes that you would change if you could and will if you can.

There's nothing wrong with thinking that way, except of course that it's completely wrong. It might be right if it weren't for God and what he tells us, but there is God, and he has spoken.

In the Bible this guy named Paul talked about a weakness he hated and begged God to remove from his life. You would think that God, being love and all, would say, "Yes! Sure, of course I will." But that's not what God, being love and all, actually said. He denied Paul's request, saying, "My grace is sufficient for you, for my power is made perfect in weakness."[2]

So how does Paul react? Does he insist that God is wrong and again beg him to take it away? Does he whine about how he's serving God and look what God gave in return?

Nope.

Paul says, "Therefore I will boast all the more gladly about my weaknesses, so that Christ's power may rest on me. That is why, for Christ's sake, I delight in weaknesses, in insults, in hardships, in persecutions, in difficulties. For when I am weak, then I am strong."[3]

And there's nothing sensible about thinking this way, except of course that it's completely right.

Paul learned the Gerald McBoing Boing lesson. See, it turns out that Gerald's weakness never stopped being his weakness, but later it became his greatest strength. What happens is this dude comes along and finds Gerald (who is carrying one of those hobo bags on the end of a stick) at a train station. This guy looks a lot like Colonel Mustard from the game Clue and is wearing a long, yellow trench coat. Now, I have specifically taught my kids to run *screaming* from guys who look like Colonel Mustard in long trench coats, but Gerald didn't have such good parenting. (His father and mother did, after all, disown him simply because he kept saying, "Boing. Boing.") Colonel Mustard guy says, "My boy, I have searched for you many long weeks!" (Run, Gerald, run!) And then he explains why: he owns the Bong-Bong-Bong radio station and needs someone who can make all kinds of noises.[4] Gerald agrees; as a six-year-old hobo, he doesn't have a lot of options. And pretty soon, we're told, "Gerald is rich, he has friends, he's well fed, 'cause he doesn't speak words, but goes Boing Boing instead!"

See, Paul learned the Gerald McBoing Boing lesson. He learned to embrace his weakness and see that God could turn it into his greatest strength. He discovered that he had a loving God who wants us to have something in our lives that we can't control, because if we're in control of everything, we have less need for God. He learned that when we're needy, we run to God. That when we're weak, we're forced to hold tight to him. And that when we do great things out of our *weaknesses*, it's God (not us) who gets the glory.

♥

Are *you* ready to learn the Gerald McBoing Boing lesson? What are your weaknesses and wounds? And what is your attitude toward them? Is it possible you're not the guerrilla lover you want to be because you've been trying to operate strictly out of your strengths, but God wants to show up in your life (minus the trench coat) and empower your weaknesses?

Listen to Paul again:

> When I came to you, brothers, I did not come with eloquence or superior wisdom as I proclaimed to you the testimony about God. For I resolved to know nothing while I was with you except Jesus Christ and him crucified. I came to you in weakness and fear, and with much trembling. My message and my preaching were not with wise and persuasive words, but with a demonstration of the Spirit's power, so that your faith might not rest on men's wisdom, but on God's power.[5]

See, Paul surrendered his weakness to God's power, and it became a strength from which he was able to minister to others.

I've experienced this as well. When I decided to become a pastor, I believed my greatest weakness was my background. I didn't come from a Christian home. In fact, I had an abusive father. I hadn't been a believer for a long time, and I only attended seminary for nine months. But to my surprise, here it is fourteen years later, and I would say my background is the greatest strength of my ministry. It's allowed me to relate to people with less than pristine histories and a lack of Christian credentials. It's also allowed them to relate to me. One time in a message I told about a time when my father was pretty cruel to my mother and me. One lady who had been coming consistently for four years had her husband with her that day. He would consent to going with her a few times a year. As they walked out that morning he said, "Okay, I'll come every week now."

"What?" she asked. "Really? Why?"

It turns out that his father was a lot like mine. "I didn't know Vince's father was like that," he explained. "I can relate to him now. Now I'll listen to him."

I mentioned earlier that my wife has also learned the Gerald McBoing Boing lesson. Her greatest weakness has been her ongoing battle with depression. Her greatest strength has been . . . her ongoing battle with depression. It has not only taught her to be dependent on God day by day but also provided her countless opportunities to speak into the lives of other women who share her struggle.

I have a friend whose teenage daughter died in a car accident. I'll never forget the pain of watching him sit in his living room just hours after it happened and the pain of seeing his tortured face at the funeral. And I will never forget the power of watching him sit with people experiencing a similar tragedy and the special way he was able to ease some of their pain at the funeral. His most pronounced weakness has become his most pronounced strength.

I have another friend who wrestled with a pornography addiction. He prayed for instant freedom from its grasp, but his healing was anything but immediate. His battle for liberation led him back again and again into counseling and support groups. He read books and articles. His inability to overcome his addiction with a single prayer or through sheer willpower forced him to become an expert in understanding addiction to pornography, and he now ministers to dozens of guys who are addicted to pornography.

Can you say Gerald McBoing Boing?

And so, again, what about you? Where have you been wounded? What are your weaknesses? And how, through God's power, can they become your strengths?

Perhaps you're divorced and feel like a failure. You can never seem to fit in, because people are either married or single but young. Could it be that God wants to take that weakness and make it your strength? Maybe his plan is to bring healing to your life, show you clearly what went wrong, and allow you to someday lead a divorce recovery support group.

Or maybe you're unable to have a child. And it hurts. But what would it look like to give that hurt to God and allow him to make you strong? It's a process; it won't happen overnight. But what if God gave you love and energy to pour into kids in the children's ministry of your church, or to pair up with a single mom and really help out with her children, or to adopt a child who otherwise has no chance at hope?

Or maybe you've struggled with an eating disorder and God is calling you to see his power at work in that area so that you will eventually experience a victory through his strength. Keep at it; don't give up. Sooner than you ever dreamed possible, you might be able to minister to people who share that same struggle.

For you it might be something different altogether: your learning disability, your time in prison, that drug addiction you had back in college, the stutter you had as a child that still occasionally comes out at the most inopportune moments.

For real, what about you? Where are you wounded? What are your weaknesses? And is it possible that they are actually your greatest strengths? What might that strength look like? Perhaps Thornton Wilder was right: "In Love's service, only wounded soldiers can serve."[6]

It's Time to Talk Guerrilla

Eric Moussamboni is from the small country of Equatorial Guinea. When Eric was twenty years old, he got to be in the Olympics. The only pool in his country available for training was only 20 meters long. Eric was only given access to it occasionally, when the president of the Olympic Federation from his country would come to let him in to train. But still, Eric was elected to represent his country in the 100 meter swim, though he had never swam a hundred meters in a row and had barely trained at all.

In his Olympic heat for the 100 meter, the gun went off, and both the other swimmers he was competing against were disqualified for a false start. Eric Moussamboni was now swimming in the Olympic pool *alone*. "Swimming" may be an exaggeration; it was closer to a doggie paddle. As he finally made it about halfway, the crowd of 17,000 people started to root for him because he was really struggling. He eventually, and barely, finished with his 100 meters, clocking in at 1:52. That was 55 seconds slower than the next slowest guy!

After the race he was barely able to pull himself out of the pool but received a standing ovation when he did. A reporter immediately asked how he felt, and Eric said, "This is the biggest day of my life. I finished a 100 meters, and I'm going to go back and find my mom, and we're going to sing and dance."

1. Do you, like Eric Moussamboni, have a goal that seems beyond your ability? If so, what is it?
2. Eric didn't have what he needed for training and may have lacked necessary athletic ability. What do you have going *against* you in your dream of reaching your goal or just becoming a guerrilla lover in general?
3. What do you think about the idea presented in this chapter (and in the Bible in 2 Corinthians 12:9–10) that our true strength lies in the place of our greatest weakness? How can that be true? Have you ever experienced that in your life?
4. Eric Moussamboni persevered even in the face of obstacles. What would help you to continue moving forward to your goal and a life of guerrilla love, even in the face of your weaknesses and struggles?
5. In the end, Eric celebrated. When was the last time you celebrated something God has done through you? And how do you picture the final celebration God has for all his guerrilla lovers?

It's Time to Get Guerrilla

In this chapter the questions were asked: "Where have you been wounded? What are your weaknesses? And how, through

wer, can they become your strength?" Why don't you
...e time to prayerfully answer those questions?

1. Where have you been wounded?
2. What are your weaknesses?
3. How, through God's power, can they become your strength?
4. God does not want to waste the pain you've gone through, and he's totally capable of asserting his strength in your place of weakness. So why not take some time to make a commitment to God right now that you'll allow him to do that?
5. What particular wounding or weakness do you want to invite God to redeem and use for his kingdom?
6. What holy experiment could you try that would allow God to start working in your life in that way?
7. If you can't think of anything, ask a trusted friend to help you. Explain to them the concept of this chapter and that you're looking for some struggles you've been through that God could use to make you into a wounded soldier. Ask your friend to help you identify what that might be and a plan for acting on it.

For more assignments and ideas, and to learn about and become a part of the Guerrilla Lover movement, go to www .guerrillalovers.com.

14

ANTI-TERROR RESOURCES

Have you ever thought about how much money terrorists spend to change the world? Probably not, but it turns out terrorism isn't cheap. Guns and bombs don't come free. I've read that the 9/11 attacks cost about $500,000. Driven by hate, terrorists will live below their means so that they can invest their excess in hating the world.

Isn't that crazy?

But what's even more startling is that Christians, who are supposed to be driven by love, won't spend their money to change the world. The statistics tells us that Christians, on average, give about 2 percent of their income to church. They don't give any more than non-Christians to the poor or other charities. They tend to live (as do non-Christians) slightly *above* their means, counting on credit cards to cover the difference.

Now that's *really* crazy.

It reminds me of a story Jesus told in the Bible. Jesus talks about a guy he describes as "a rich man."[1] Apparently he already has an abundance, and his land is once again producing a bumper crop. He asks himself, "What shall I do? I have no place to store my crops."[2] He decides to tear down his barns because, though they're loaded with excess crops, still they don't hold *enough* excess. He needs barns that will hold even more excess. So he tears down his barns and builds bigger ones. He looks forward to the day his project will be completed so he can, "take life easy; eat, drink and be merry."[3] But on the day he finishes building his barns, he dies. And God enters the story, calling the man a "fool."[4] I understand that the exact word Jesus used means "no brain." God says, "You've lived like you don't have the brains I gave you. You've been a fool. This is the day your life ends. And you're not going to enjoy all that you've saved for yourself." Then Jesus gives a warning: "This is how it will be with anyone who stores up things for himself but is not rich toward God."[5]

So why was this guy a fool? I like what Andy Stanley proposes in his book *It Came From Within*.[6] The reason this guy was a no-brain is because he asked the wrong question. Instead of, "What should I do with my extra?" he should have asked, "Why do I have so much?"

And we need to ask that same question.

Now you might be wondering, "What do you mean, why do I have so much? I don't have enough! I don't have as much as I want!" And, really, who does? We all have a wish list of things we don't have. But think for a moment about all you *do* have. My guess is that every person who reads this book has *way* more than most of the people in the world.

Jesus said the guy in the story was a rich man, but I bet he didn't think of himself as rich. He could name other people who had more, and how could he be rich if other people had more? But Jesus says, "No, he was rich. He had more than he needed."

And if Jesus told a story about you, I bet he would call you a rich man or woman. You may not think of yourself as rich. You can name other people who have more, so how can you be rich if other people have more? But Jesus would say, "No, you are rich. You have more than you need."

That's because when Jesus looks at you and what you have, he doesn't see you in comparison to people on *Lifestyles of the Rich and Famous* or even in your neighborhood. Jesus sees the whole world, and in that context, you and I are rich.

Did you know there are about 6 billion people in the world? Americans make up less than 6 percent of the world's population, but we consume about 50 percent of the world's resources. Or check this out: the average American consumes in a year the same amount as 520 Ethiopians do.

When you look outside America, here's some of what you'll see:

- 1.2 billion people in the world don't have access to clean water. (Do you have access to clean water?)
- One billion people live in extreme poverty—meaning their access to food, water, and shelter is so limited that death constantly hangs over them. In fact, about every three seconds someone in the world dies because they don't have enough food. (As you read this book, is your big question "What's for dinner tonight?" or "Will I live long enough to finish this chapter?")
- 80 percent of the people of the world live in substandard housing.
- 70 percent of the world is unable to read.
- Only 1 percent of the people of the world have a college education.
- Only 8 percent of the people in the world own a car. (So if you own one car, you're richer than 92 percent of the world! If your family owns two cars, well, you figure it out.)
- Or how about this: if you have spare money somewhere, anywhere—you have something in the bank, a few bucks

in your wallet, or a jar full of change at home—then you are in the richest 8 percent of the world.

So, are you rich?

If so, the question to ask is, "*Why do I have so much?*" Or to put it another way, "Why has God provided me with more than I need?"

In his book, Andy Stanley goes through some possibilities. Maybe God has provided you with more than you need so you can make sure your children have everything they need. But I doubt it. Giving your children a lot of money doesn't typically set them up for success, and in fact, it can cause a variety of problems for them. (Insert your own Paris Hilton joke here.)

Or perhaps God has provided you with an abundance so you don't have to worry? That's probably not it either. The Bible says that contentment and peace are supposed to come from God, not our money. And people who have more really don't tend to worry less; they just have more to worry about.

Or God could have given you more so you can elevate your standard of living. But I don't think so. The Bible talks about money and possessions more than just about any other topic, and a multitude of verses warn about greed, spending all you have on yourself, and not caring for those in need, but I have not yet seen a Bible verse about using God's money to improve your lifestyle and make sure you're comfortable.

Another possibility is that maybe God has given you extra so you can save and retire early. But this option doesn't ring true for me either. In fact, in Jesus's story, that's what the rich man seems to be saving for—early retirement. And God calls him a fool.

So what's the answer? Why do you have so much? Why has God provided you with more than you need?

Stanley writes, "Remember what your mother told you when you had two cookies and your sister had none? 'Quick, eat 'em both before she can wrench one out of your greedy little hands!' Probably not. She would say, 'Share.'"[7]

Think about this: what if you were watching a child eat two cookies in the presence of another child who had none? That wouldn't seem right, would it? What if it was three cookies? What if it was four? I think you'd feel compelled to say something. I think you'd have to do something. I think you'd tell that child, "You need to share."

I'll take it a step further. Picture a hundred kids and a hundred cookies, but six of the kids have fifty of the cookies, more than eight each, while the other ninety-four kids have fifty cookies to share between them. So they barely get half a cookie each. A lot of them don't have any cookie at all, or maybe just some crumbs.

That's the world we live in. *And you're the kid with eight or nine cookies.* What do you think God would say to you? Why do you think God has provided you with more than you need? Why do you have so much?

I think the answer is *to share.*

God wants us to share. He's given us more than we need so we can care for the needs of others.

What if we actually obeyed God? What if we took him seriously? What if we viewed our excess as God-given resources to meet people's needs and fund Jesus's revolution? What if we shared in a way that drew others into the revolution?

The first Christians clearly understood this. Check out the first snapshots we get of our revolutionary ancestors:

> All the believers were together and had everything in common. Selling their possessions and goods, they gave to anyone as he had need.[8]

> All the believers were one in heart and mind. No one claimed that any of his possessions was his own, but they shared

everything they had. . . . There were no needy persons among them. For from time to time those who owned lands or houses sold them, brought the money from the sales and put it at the apostles' feet, and it was distributed to anyone as he had need.[9]

What were they doing? They were sharing.

And what was happening? Acts 2:47 reports that they enjoyed "the favor of all the people. And the Lord added to their number daily those who were being saved."

We live in a world where Christianity has a black eye (and a beer gut). But when you see people making sacrifices to meet the needs of others, there's something attractive and undeniable about it. There's no argument against that. It's magnetic; you want to be a part of something like that.

So what if we shared? What if we chose to no longer live above our means? What if we chose to live *below* our means so that we could share more and make a greater difference in changing the world? What if we used our money to become guerrilla lovers?

If we choose to do this, one huge difference it will make will be in *us*.

In the last few years I have made a decent amount of money, and I have spent it in all kinds of ways. Two years ago I bought my first iPod. Last year I bought a newer car. The contents of my closet prove I've spent some money on clothes and shoes. But to be honest, I can't remember how it *felt* to purchase any of those items. They were all things I was excited to buy and felt like I "needed," but actually acquiring them gave me no rush.

Let me tell you what did.

On two different occasions in the past few months, my wife and I decided to give some extra money away. Both times we knew of a family in need and realized that some of our extra could meet their need. So each time we told our kids what we were going to do, filled an envelope with hundred dollar bills, and drove over to the home of the family. We wanted our act of kindness to remain a secret, so the whole way over we discussed how we could drop off the money undetected. The kids were getting more and more excited but tried to whisper (I'm not sure why; maybe they think our car is bugged). Finally, nearing the house, we turned off our headlights and parked behind a tree. I quietly opened my door and then ran toward the house, keeping cover behind bushes and parked cars. I slid the envelope under the welcome mat and then ran back to the car. I gently closed the door, put the car in reverse, turned it around, and then sped away, everyone in the family celebrating that we had not been caught and imagining how the family would react when they found the envelope.

That was a rush. I can't think about it without smiling. But the other ways I've spent my money, well, they just don't do anything for me.

And check this: the first time we did a give-money sneak ambush, as we drove away, the radio station we were already listening to started playing "Guerrilla Radio" by Rage Against the Machine. I'm not kidding. We drove away with the lyrics pumping, "Lights out. Guerrilla radio!" Then the singer whispered, "It has to start somewhere. It has to start sometime. What better place than here? What better time than now?"

That was fun!

When we choose to use our extra to become guerrilla lovers, it changes *us*.

One of the churches in America that seems to really understand this is Vineyard Community Church in Cincinnati. In his book *The Outward-Focused Life*, their pastor David Workman shares an email he received from someone who had just become a believer:

> Today was fun. It was a normal workday in most senses, but I decided to do things a little differently. It was time to start

serving people in the name of the Lord. I went to several different accounts for work today. I looked around and was able to locate a soda machine at a few of them. I made sure that no one was around, and I began purchasing some cans of pop. I rubber-banded a connect card from our church to each soda and placed them back in the dispenser slot. I noticed that pretty much every pop machine will allow three cans of soda to sit in the dispenser. $1.50 can show three people that God loves them! After I secretly placed the cans in the dispenser, I went on to my daily routines. I couldn't help but spy a little bit and check back to see if anyone had taken a soda. To my surprise, the sodas were gone almost immediately!

As I was walking by, I saw a woman who looked like she was having a bad day. She grabbed one of the "free" sodas from the machine and began reading the connect card. She looked as if she had just been thrown a life preserver. I felt a lump in my throat immediately, and I had to turn away.

I noticed today that this thing is more addictive than crack cocaine. I couldn't wait to do more and more of it. I ran up to the grocery store, and while walking by the quarter gumball machines, I had an idea. I set a connect card on the top of each machine and placed a quarter on every one of them. By the time I was leaving the grocery store, there was only one card left. I feel like I'm on fire! I already invited a group to do the outreach on Saturday morning. This is the life Jesus promises!

Sincerely,

Ryan[10]

Then Workman writes:

A few weeks ago I was on an outreach, heading to a Section 8 housing complex to hand out little boxes of Tide detergent. A youth group from another church in town had joined us. I didn't know their youth pastor, who was tattooed with a few piercings and was teamed up with me. As we drove to the place, he told me that when he was younger, he was deep into partying, drugs, living with his girlfriend, and being your basic hell-raiser.

But four different times he was approached by people who offered him a free bottle of water, washed his car, gave him a free Coke, etc. Four times. For months he hung on to the little card that was given to him, and finally he decided to check out the church.

It was there that he met Jesus after going through our Alpha program. And now he's serving in ministry as a youth pastor in another church, teaching students how to give their lives away in servanthood.

So as we were driving to the outreach he said to me, "I sent you an e-mail years ago . . . about attaching cards to pop cans where I worked. My name is Ryan."[11]

If we choose to use our extra to become guerrilla lovers, the other huge difference it will make will be in *those around us*. In his book, Workman shares another email he received:

Dear Dave,

After growing up surrounded by hypocritical Christian examples and attending college philosophy classes, I became an atheist, and the worst kind too. I frequently antagonized Christians, even claiming to be the antichrist just to see them flush.

Years later I moved to Cincinnati. One night, a guy handed me a Starbucks free-coffee card with Vineyard information on it. He walked away without saying a word. Scoffing at the "church gunk" but never turning down free Starbucks, I kept the card.

It was months before I redeemed it. The following morning, I jumped up and went to the 8:30 a.m. Vineyard Celebration. I cannot explain it! I hated mornings even more than Christians! I was pleasantly surprised, even for an atheist, to see people who lived what they spoke. The non-pushy environment enticed me to come the next week . . . and the next. I've been coming back for nine years now . . . though I do prefer the 11:30 a.m. service.

Sincerely, Bill[12]

That's crazy! All it took was one guerrilla lover who was willing to part with a few extra dollars, enough to buy a Starbucks gift card, and hand the card to a stranger. When we choose to use our extra to become love terrorists, it changes *those around us*.

A few years back outdoor-sports writer Jim Robey wrote an article in the *Dayton Daily News*. He began with, "People say miracles never happen. I'm a believer now, thanks to someone I never met." Robey had been in line at a Subway restaurant when a mother and daughter, who were standing in front of him, paid his bill. He was stunned and stopped at their table on his way out to thank them. He writes:

> "That was kind of you to pay for my lunch, but here, take this," I said, handing them money for the sandwich.
>
> "No," the mother insisted. "It's something I want to do. . . . We go to the Vineyard Church on Indian Ripple Road [and] lately we've been talking in church about doing for others," the mother explained.
>
> "Well, no stranger ever offered to buy my lunch before. I don't know what to say, other than thank you."
>
> What's shocking is being on the receiving end of generosity. It's miraculous. . . . I can't imagine buying lunch for my hunting and fishing buddies, let alone someone I don't know.
>
> Heretofore, I have proclaimed to my friends that my most valuable service to humanity has been to rise early, set forth with rod and gun and bless the waters, the woods and the fields for all. So far, no one has been impressed.
>
> I must find something more. What a better world it would be if everyone expressed kindness to a total stranger. It may not be buying a stranger's lunch, but there are countless other ways. I'm thinking about them. . . .
>
> To our readers who expect information on outdoor topics when they look at this space, excuse the diversion. A miracle could not go unnoticed.[13]

Again, all it took was one guerrilla lover who was willing to part with a little of her extra, enough to buy a sub for a stranger. When we choose to use our extra to become love terrorists, it changes *those around us.*

♥

Why do we have so much? Why has God provided us with more than we need? What if we shared? What if we chose to live below our means so that we could share more and make a greater difference in changing the world? What if we used our money to become love terrorists?

Can you hear it? Can you hear the lyrics? I'm not sure, but I think it's God singing:

> It has to start somewhere
> It has to start sometime
> What better place than here?
> What better time than now?

It's Time to Talk Guerrilla

1. Do you remember being told as a child to share? Who taught you that lesson? What were you most often told to share?
2. How did the statistics about the financial situation of many in the world versus the economic prosperity of almost all Americans make you feel? Why?
3. What did you think about the cookie metaphor? Does it make sense to you? Do you agree with it? How did it make you feel?
4. Let's talk about the questions posed in this chapter: Why do you have so much? Why has God provided you with more than you need?
5. The passages from Acts chapters 2 and 4 show clearly that the first Christians shared their resources. How have you seen Christians today share in that kind of way?

6. Have you ever been the recipient of such sharing or had the opportunity to share your resources with someone in a way that really made a difference? If so, how did that make you feel?
7. What is the most impressive example of generosity you've ever seen?
8. What do you think keeps most people from sharing their resources?
9. What do you think most keeps *you* from sharing your resources?
10. What in this chapter most makes you feel like you really want to start sharing your resources?
11. What changes would you need to make to start living below your means instead of above your means?
12. How does the idea of becoming "love terrorists" sit with you?
13. Discuss this quote from Shane Claiborne, author of *The Irresistible Revolution*: "If we are crazy, then it is because we refuse to be crazy in the same way that the world has gone crazy. . . . After all, what is crazier: one person owning the same amount of money as the combined economies of twenty-three countries, or suggesting that if we shared, there would be enough for everyone?"

It's Time to Get Guerrilla

So are you ready to get serious about this? It's going to be difficult, because you have the same problem that every human being has: you are selfish. We all are. We want to spend our money on ourselves. But deep down we know life has a purpose greater than our own. Deep down we know we can do something better with our money than spend it on upgrading our toys and buying things we want but don't really need.

So why not make a decision right now to stop living above your means and start intentionally living *below* your means?

If you're currently in debt, you may have to take some steps to get out of your financial hole. A variety of resources can help you with that (for instance, check out www.daveram sey.com, www.outofdebtchristian.com, or www.goodsense ministry.com).

Why not respond to this chapter by choosing to live below your means? Start by making a commitment to give 10 percent of your income to your church and/or other causes you feel God is leading you to support (see Proverbs 3:5, 9; Leviticus 27:30; Deuteronomy 14:23; Malachi 3:8–10; Matthew 23:23).

But let's take it one step further. What if you chose to live another $1,040 per year below your means so you had $20 a week to fund your work as a love terrorist? If you had a budget of $20 every week to serve people, love people, touch people's lives, and make this world a little bit better place, what could you do?

You may have no idea right now, but if you had that specially designated $20 in your pocket, opportunities would start to pop out at you. The days when you spent some or all of that $20 to serve and make someone's day better—those would be the best days of your week. And you wouldn't be sorry you didn't spend that money on yourself.

For more assignments and ideas, and to learn about and become a part of the Guerrilla Lover movement, go to www .guerrillalovers.com.

LIPSTICK GRAFFITI

One of my favorite friends is James. I like James for a lot of reasons, but mostly because he's entertaining, and I love to be entertained. One of the amusing things about James is that he's one of those guys you want to ask, "Are you aware that you're white?" My daughter, at the age of five, would occasionally strut around our house like Shaft going, "I'm James. Yo man, what up, what up, what up?" and throwing peace signs in every direction.

One time a bunch of us were at a baseball game and James made some theological point he considered deep, then said, "You know, I have been called a modern-day C. S. Lewis." Everyone started laughing and James protested, "I have!" When pressed, James finally told us who gave him this moniker: he did. He calls himself a modern-day C. S. Lewis.

At his wedding, James wore a tux jacket that went all the way down to his ankles. It was a totally *Matrix* wedding.

Another time I was with a bunch of people from my church feeding homeless people. I was with this homeless guy who was about my age and in some ways seemed to have his act together and have reasonable social skills. But something was very sad about his eyes; they had no life in them. I was trying to figure out how to start a conversation with him when James strolled up, looked him in the eye, and said, "So, dude, what's your drug of choice?"

What the . . . ?

But the homeless guy sighed and told James his drug of choice. James started boldly asking questions: "When did you start doing that? Why did you start? Why can't you stop? Do you have a job? What if we found someone who would receive your paycheck and only give you funds when you need them to make sure you didn't blow the whole thing?"

I was just staring at James, entertained but also a little in awe. Then I looked over at the homeless guy, and he was agreeing and nodding, and I'm pretty sure I saw a little flicker of something—excitement, hope, life, soul?—in his eyes.

It was like just through asking a few questions, James gave him back a hint of his humanity.

Why am I telling you about my friend James? Because one day he started talking a lot about Banksy. "I love Banksy." "Banksy is the greatest." Well, I assumed that James must have gotten a new cat named Banksy, so when I heard James say something about how Banksy was having a major impact on the world, I was like, "Dude, seriously. I'm sorry, but your cat is *not* changing the world. He's just not."

That's when I found out Banksy isn't a cat.

Banksy, it turns out, is an artist. He's a guerrilla graffiti artist.

Banksy is the most well-known unknown graffiti artist in the world. Many people know his art, some even buy his art (Brad Pitt and Angelina Jolie recently spent $2 million on some of his graffiti), but no one knows who he is. People speculate about his identity, but they can only guess. Banksy is allegedly from England but works all over the world. He goes out under cover of night and creates his graffiti masterpieces in strategic spots. Generally his work tells a story or makes a statement. He takes boring, drab scenery and adds creativity and beauty with his ideas.

For instance, Banksy painted a dove (the symbol of peace) wearing a bulletproof vest with crosshairs over its chest on a wall in Israel. And after Hurricane Katrina ravaged New Orleans, Banksy came in and left amazing paintings around the city.

While police must, by necessity, consider Banksy's work vandalism, the art community views his graffiti as master-pieces to be treasured. Probably more importantly, his art inspires people to think and adds value to their neighbor-hoods. It does something to their souls.

What is it that drives Banksy? Banksy answers this question by telling the following story:

> Lieutenant Colonel Mervin Willet Gonin DSO was among the first British soldiers to liberate the Bergen-Belsen Nazi Concentration Camp in 1945. Gonin and others who went in to liberate the camp describe the barren human wilderness they found with horrific words. Corpses lay everywhere. Ema-ciated ghost-like people wandered around aimlessly. Moth-ers carried their dead babies as if they were still alive. Most of both the dead and living were naked. People ate worms and dirt to try and stay alive. Women washed themselves in a tank of water that also contained the floating bodies of dead children.
>
> Shortly after the British Red Cross arrived to liberate the camp and try to help save lives and lead people back to health, a very strange shipment arrived. What you would expect is . . . medicine, food, vitamins, bandages. But no, what was delivered to the camp was a large quantity of . . . lipstick. Gonin, who was there to help, says that at first the shipment made him furious, but soon he saw it as an act of "genius, sheer unadulterated brilliance. I believe nothing did more for these internees than the lipstick. Women lay in bed with no sheets and no nightie but with scarlet red lips . . . At last someone had done something to make them individu-

als again, they were someone, no longer merely the number tattooed on the arm. At last they could take an interest in their appearance. That lipstick started to give them back their humanity."[1]

At that concentration camp it was tubes of lipstick. For Banksy, it's some fresh paint on a wall in a hurricane-devastated or war-torn city that starts to give people back their humanity.

In some sense what we're trying to do as guerrilla lovers is give people back their humanity. Ultimately, we hope to connect people to God, who is the source of humanity. According to the Bible, man didn't become human until God breathed his Spirit into man. Until that moment he was just the stuff of earth, kind of like Pinocchio before he became a real boy. But when God breathes his Spirit into Adam, he becomes something different than anything else, something special; he becomes human.

I've noticed that only humans can respond to and connect with God. Have you noticed that? I mean, I've dunked my dog under water, but he's never come up singing "Amazing Grace." I can invest hours of my life discipling a plunger, but it's never going to get its life out of the toilet. (That has to be the worst joke I've ever told. Sorry.)

We're trying to lead people to respond to God, to connect to God, but some of these people have become less than human. Life has had its way with them, and it's left them in a subhuman place.

So perhaps the first thing we need to do is restore people's humanity. That might sound difficult, but James did it by asking some questions. Banksy does it with graffiti art. Someone else did it with tubes of lipstick. Perhaps it's not that difficult after all. Maybe people just need to be loved back into their humanity, and maybe it can be done in all kinds of ways.

♥

I decided to follow Jesus as a sophomore in college. At the time I was working part time at a movie theater. I worked with a sad girl who had hollow eyes. Her name was Jennifer, and it seemed like it was just too much work for her to smile. She seemed to have somehow misplaced her humanity.

I could relate to that, to feeling like I was less than I was meant to be. But I had found something that changed all that. And so more than anything I wanted to spring Jesus on her. I wanted to tell her, "He's the solution to that problem you're constantly trying to figure out in your head: Why doesn't this add up? Why do I have so much but feel like I'm missing something significant?" I wanted to just walk up to her and say, "Jesus. The answer is Jesus."

But I didn't.

Somehow it didn't seem like the right first move, even though I knew ultimately Jesus was the answer to her problems. Later I heard a quote from William Booth, the guy who founded the Salvation Army, about how a man can't really hear the gospel if he's in pain from a toothache. That makes sense. And my instincts said that springing Jesus on this sad girl didn't make sense as the first step. First I needed to address her toothache. First I needed to help restore her humanity.

So instead of offering what she really needed, I bought her a candy necklace. You know, those candy necklaces you wore and ate as a kid? Remember nibbling off the multicolored little candies circling the elastic string? Well, I was in a convenience store just before work one day, saw a candy necklace, and thought, *Maybe that would cheer Jennifer up. Maybe it would make her feel special, knowing that someone thought of her when she wasn't around, like she was worthy of receiving a present.*

I have no idea why, but I saw the candy necklace and it spoke to me. Actually, the price tag was what spoke to me. I think the necklace cost seventy-nine cents. Seventy-nine cents was squarely within my budget.

Ten minutes later I walked up to Jennifer and said, "Hey, I was thinking of you, so I got you something." I handed her the candy necklace. Her sad eyes got big, and for the first time I saw them shine.

"You got this for me?" she asked.

"Yeah."

"But why?"

"I don't know," I told her. "I just thought you might like it."

"I love it." She was beaming.

"Well, don't have it appraised," I said. "It's not real."

I also decided if I could get her laughing, she would feel more human. Jennifer sold tickets from a glass-enclosed alcove. The acoustics were amazing in there, a little echo chamber. So at every opportunity I went in and sang "Immigrant Song" by Led Zeppelin at the top of my lungs. I did this time after time, day after day, week after week. If that won't cheer someone up, I don't know what will.

Our theater often had stacks of coupons available ("Buy a large popcorn and drink, get a small candy free!"), and I would write Jen insane notes on them. "Why are Goobers called Goobers? Isn't that prejudiced?" "Have you seen *Sister Act* yet? It's playing in theater 5, and it is totally nun-tastic. It's the feel-nun movie of the year." "If I drown Greg in the popcorn bin, do you think I could get away with it?" "I feel so sexy in this polyester uniform. People laugh at us in all this polyester, but they have no idea what it does to you on the inside. I am a sexy beast in this vest!" "I just watched the end of *Home Alone 2*. Don't worry, the kid lives." "*Junior* Mints? Where's the father, that's what I want to know!"

Finally, after months of me brightening Jennifer's days, Jennifer spoke the words I had been waiting for. She said, "I wish I was more like you."

During my break I wrote her a letter explaining that I didn't used to be this way; not long ago I was sad and vacant and confused, but finding a real relationship with God through Jesus had changed everything for me. I had become something very different because of Jesus. And what I was, was a Christian.

That night Jennifer left a message on my answering machine: "Whatever you are, that's what I want to be."

Several times over the next few weeks, we got together at a restaurant, and I would share with her what I had learned about Jesus, how to begin a relationship with Jesus, and what it was like to do life with Jesus.

After a bunch of conversations and reading the Bible, Jennifer decided she wanted Jesus in her life too.

She changed *dramatically*. Bright eyes, a playful smile on her face. It was like she had come alive. Like she was a real person again; like she was given back her humanity.

And, by the way, she later became my wife. Score!

One of the goals of guerrilla love is to restore people's humanity. To get them to a place where they can respond to and connect with God. And restoring a person's humanity may seem like a bigger task than you're capable of, but it's not. It doesn't have to be vast and expensive and beyond our ability. It doesn't need to be something you can't do; in fact, it needs to be something you *can* do. Something you have, some ability you possess, something you can give which seems utterly insignificant but when used in love's service can have significance beyond reason.

Perhaps you could start making your special recipe soup for your neighbors. Maybe getting something good to eat out of nowhere will make them feel special for the first time in a long time.

Or maybe you have a car you're not using.

You know that your coworker's favorite candy is Peanut M&M's.

You're good at wallpapering.

You understand the fundamentals of a good golf swing.

You have a green thumb.

You speak a second language.

Perhaps you have Tuesday nights free, and your single mother neighbor could use an evening away from her kids once a week.

What could you do to put a sparkle in a person's eye, make them laugh again, help them feel worth someone's attention?

I love the story my friend John Burke shares from a woman in his church in Austin, Texas:

My neighbor came to faith after getting to know some of the women in our neighborhood who threw a welcome party for her family when they moved in. She wanted her husband to find faith too, but he was a very stoic, skeptical intellectual. For months and months, our husbands would try to grapple with his deep questions as they dialogued about faith, but nothing could convince him, it seemed. One day I was in the garden, praying for him as I knew it was his birthday. As I prayed for him, I felt prompted to pick a red rose to give to him with a birthday card. I was actually quite intimidated by him, so I took the rose early in the morning and taped it to his front door with a card that simply said, "Love you, and so does God." Shortly after that, he became a Christ-follower, and they started coming to church. Several years later, I was talking to him, and he said, "You don't know this, but the reason I opened my heart to Christ was because of the rose you left me on my birthday—I'd never been given a flower before in my life, and for some reason, God's love for me struck my heart for the first time when I got that rose. It was the factor that opened me to faith."[2]

It's Time to Talk Guerrilla

1. What would you say makes a human, human? In other words, what makes a human different from a cat?

2. Read Genesis 1:1–3. The Old Testament is written in Hebrew, and the word used for the Spirit of God in verse 2 is *ruah*. *Ruah* can mean wind, or air, or breath, or Spirit of God. Read Genesis 2:7. After forming man out of the dust of the ground, God breathes into his nostrils the breath of life, and the man becomes a human being. The Hebrew word used for "breath" in 2:7 is, again, *ruah*. The *ruah* that was hovering over the earth is now breathed into man, making him human and making him in the image of God.

3. What do you think about this idea that it's the very Spirit of God that makes a person human? How does it make you feel? What does it say to you about humans?

4. In the creation account, humans are the only creatures that God breathes his Spirit into. This is why only humans can have a relationship with God, and why only humans have a soul.

5. The Bible teaches throughout the New Testament that when a person decides to give their life to God and follow Jesus, he or she receives the gift of the Spirit. If having the Spirit breathed into us is what made us human, why do you think we need to have the Spirit breathed into us again when we come to Christ?

6. The Bible also speaks of the idea that a Christian can quench or put out the Spirit (see for instance 1 Thessalonians 5:19). How do you think that's possible?

7. So what do you think of the idea presented in this chapter that perhaps part of the reason people who are far from God can't connect with him is because they have quenched the Spirit and his work in their lives (and have thus become something less than human)?

8. If there is any truth to that idea, would it make sense that perhaps the first thing we need to do for such a person is help restore their humanity? Why?

9. Thinking about what makes a human a human, what are some ways you could help restore someone's humanity?

It's Time to Get Guerrilla

Take a moment to pray this through: who is someone you know who seems to have lost their humanity? I mean someone who, when you spend time with them or listen to them, just seems to have had the human spark God put in each of us snuffed out.

Remember the scene in *Castaway* when Tom Hanks was trying to light a fire? He worked hard to get a first spark and then would work that little spark like a madman trying to get it to burst into flame.

That person you thought of—how could you create a first spark in them, and how could you work to get it to ignite? Create a strategy to help this person regain their humanity, to help them get closer to a place where they could respond to and connect with God.

Maybe think back to what makes humans uniquely human. What can humans do that a cat can't? For instance, perhaps: laugh, ask deep questions about life, discuss their feelings, or enjoy beauty.

You might center your plan on trying to get this person to do some of those things that only a human can do. Perhaps you can guerrilla love them back to humanity and from there love them into a relationship with God that they're not even open to (or perhaps not even capable of) at this moment.

Pick your person. Develop your plan. Work your plan.

For more assignments and ideas, and to learn about and become a part of the Guerrilla Lover movement, go to www .guerrillalovers.com.

16

SUBVERSIVE SERVICE

Have you noticed how a small misunderstanding can sometimes lead to massive confusion?

Like . . . When my wife and I lived near Washington, DC, she had to pick me up at Dulles airport one night. This was before 9/11, back when you could meet someone at the gate. Jen thought she was meeting me at the gate. I thought we were meeting outside the airport. Dulles has shuttle buses that run on tracks back and forth from the main terminal to the gates. So as I stood on the bus going to the terminal, Jen was in the shuttle going past me in the opposite direction. She happened to be looking at the other bus and saw me standing there. She waved furiously and pounded on the window like Dustin Hoffman in *The Graduate*, but to no avail. This was also back before cell phones. When I didn't find Jen at the main terminal, I jumped back on the shuttle to the gate, worrying that she might be there. Jen knew where I was, so she went on the bus back to the main terminal. This time I saw Jen and was trying to get her attention by jumping up and down like a man with a snapping turtle in his pants.

Unfortunately this sequence went on for another half hour before we found each other.

Or like . . . One time our family went on a little weekend getaway to the Outer Banks of North Carolina. We were driving along when I noticed a theater sign that said drive-in. We were already past it, but I couldn't stop talking about it. "A drive-in! That's awesome! I haven't been to a drive-in since I was young. Kids, tonight you're going to a drive-in for the first time!" We spent the day at the beach, and then when dusk hit we drove over to the area where I had seen the sign, but we couldn't find a drive-in. I didn't think it would be hard to find a massive screen, but we were stumped. So finally I started pulling up to locals out for walks or doing yard work and asking, "Could you tell me where the drive-in is?"

The first person said, "I don't know."

I was annoyed. "You live here and you don't know where the drive-in is?"

"Sorry," the local person responded. "I can tell you where the regular movie theater is."

"No," I said all indignantly. "We have regular theaters where we live."

The next local felt sure there was no drive-in theater.

Now I was mad. "You mean to tell me that you live here, there's a drive-in right around here somewhere, and you don't know that it exists?"

"That's right," the local guy answered. "I'm pretty sure we don't have one."

Well, at that point I was questioning the sanity and brainpower of people who live in the Outer Banks and wondering if we could kick North Carolina out of the Union. Finally, after much driving around, we found the sign that I had spotted earlier in the day and . . . it was a regular movie theater featuring the movie *Driven*, starring Sylvester Stallone and Burt Reynolds. The sign said *Driven*, not Drive-in.

Or like . . . A couple of years ago I had a new administrative assistant named Juli. On her first day she was sitting in her office, which was connected to mine. I happened to have a big bag of Whoppers, full of malted milk ball goodness. So, trying to be a nice guy and give Juli a good first day, I called to her, "Juli, do you like Whoppers?"

There was a short, awkward pause and then Juli answered, "Yes."

I said, "Cool, me too. I have a whole bag of 'em in here! Do you want some?"

There was a long, awkward pause and then Juli said, "Um, no thanks."

I felt bad that Juli didn't feel comfortable enough with me to take a few Whoppers, but I didn't let on. "Okay! Well, if you want some later, just let me know. I've got tons of them."

There was a much longer and more awkward pause and then Juli said, "Well, okay, yeah, thanks."

A half hour later Juli walked into my office, saw the bag of Whoppers on my desk, and exclaimed, "Oh! You meant Whoppers *candy*. I thought you meant Whoppers as in 'Burger King: Home of the Whopper.' I couldn't understand why you had a whole bag of them or why you thought I'd want to eat a bunch of them."

A small misunderstanding can sometimes lead to massive confusion. And it's funny when it has to do with missing each other at an airport or leads to looking for a nonexistent movie theater or your new assistant thinking you're a gluttonous lunatic.

What's not so funny is when our misunderstandings are about God, and church, and what it means to live the Christian life. When that happens, sadly it can lead not to a comedy of errors but to a tragedy.

I don't claim to be infallible, but I feel pretty confident that most Christians are living life with some serious misunderstandings.

Like . . . As Christians we seem to think that we're people who get served (by the pastor and programs of our church), but that's a misunderstanding. As Christians we are people who serve.

Or like . . . We seem to think that church is something that brings in people from the community for services, but that's a misunderstanding. The church is people who go out into the community to serve.

Or like . . . We seem to think that when we do go out into the community and serve, it has to be these great, noble, and expensive acts, but that's a misunderstanding. Yes, sometimes we're called to do things that might be impressive, but most of what changes the world seems very insignificant. I love the way Mother Teresa said it: "We can do no great things, only small things with great love."

Here's where all of this becomes a tragedy: If God's people are living far from God's dream, that is tragic. And if Jesus's church is doing life far from what Jesus died for, that is tragic.

God's dream is of a people whose lives have been revolutionized by love. Jesus died that we might go out on mission to share his love with everyone. But instead we've become Christian consumers who keep our distance from the rest of the world by bunkering down in our churches, which are more like country clubs without pools, and *that's* tragic.

If we think the world is changed only by a few rock-star pastors who do evangelistic crusades or all-star Christians who start faith-based nonprofit organizations, *that's* tragic.

But what if we corrected our misunderstandings? What if we really believed that Christians are people who have given up their right to be served and instead live to serve? What if we redefined "greatness" and believed it comes through serving? And what if we viewed church not as something that brings in people from the community for services but as people who go out into the community to serve?

What might happen?

Maybe we'd start a revolution.

One of my favorite preachers to listen to is Mike Breaux. Mike shares all kinds of great wisdom and challenges, but he's also very funny. He has kind of a folksy sense of humor, probably because he's from Kentucky. Mike shares lots of stories from his family, like the time his young son saw a lightning bug and asked, "Daddy, why do they have shiny heinies?" That's good stuff.

When Mike left as the pastor of Southland Christian Church in Lexington to go become a teaching pastor at Willow Creek Community Church, I was very curious to see who would be hired to replace him. Then they announced it would be Jon Weece, who looked to be about fourteen years old but I think was actually in his upper twenties. A lot of people questioned the church's sanity for hiring such a young guy, but Jon just went to work. He decided to focus on Matthew 5:16, where Jesus says, "In the same way, let your light shine before men, that they may see your good deeds and praise your Father in heaven." Jon had something cool to say about lightning bugs as well. He saw a lightning bug once and thought, "You don't need to be the biggest or brightest light; you just need to be the nearest light."

Well, Jon started to impress people with his maturity and wisdom, and things seemed to be going well until they cancelled Christmas. In 2005, Christmas fell on a Sunday. Southland has a Christmas Eve service every year, so they asked the question: should we have everyone come for our Christmas Eve service and then have them show up again for a Christmas morning service?

Finally they decided to cancel Christmas. (Well, not Christmas, but their Christmas services.) However, they didn't tell their people to just stay home for another serve-yourself Christmas morning. Instead they challenged their people to use Christmas morning as an opportunity to go out into the community and serve others.

One of the ideas they gave was to go to a restaurant, order something inexpensive, and then leave a ridiculously large tip for the waitress forced to work on Christmas morning. So all over town people from their church were buying cups of coffee and then leaving $100 tips. One man left $1,000 in an envelope and then snuck outside and looked through the window so he could watch the waitress's reaction. When she opened the envelope, she sat down at the table and started crying uncontrollably. What the man didn't know was that this waitress was a single mom working three jobs to raise two teenage boys. The man came back into the restaurant, gave the woman a hug, and explained that he left the tip to show her God's love. That waitress started attending their church and has since become a Christian.

One family went to a Waffle House and saw a college-age boy sitting at the table next to them. They asked why he was there by himself on Christmas morning. He explained that he was driving home for Christmas when his car broke down and that he couldn't afford to fix it. The father took out the keys to his brand-new Volvo, handed them to the young man, and said, "Take it—it's yours." The kid looked around for a hidden camera, asking, "Am I getting *Punk'd*?" The dad smiled and said, "No, this is just what Jesus's followers do." And the boy went out to the car, got in, and drove away.

One ten-year-old in the church prepared for weeks for his Christmas morning serving opportunity. He went door-to-door offering to work to raise money for a boy in his class who stood out in the playground day after day shivering in an old, tattered sweatshirt. On Christmas morning the ten-year-old showed up at his classmate's house with the brand-new coat he had purchased at the mall. He handed it to his friend, saying, "Jesus wants me to give this to you." Then he gave him the $61 he had left over and said, "Your family can spend this any way you want." Three years later, that now thirteen-year-old boy stood in a pool of water with the friend he had given the coat to and baptized him.

One little girl from the church spent her Christmas Eve baking brownies with her mother. On Christmas morning they went to the University of Kentucky and handed out brownies to international students who were stuck on campus over the holidays. One young Muslim student came up, and the little girl offered him a brownie. What she didn't know was that this student was on a three-year pilgrimage, trying to figure out what he really believed. As he ate the brownie he asked her, "Why are you doing this?"

She answered, "Because Jesus changed my life."

The answer took him by surprise. After a moment he asked, "Can I come to your church?"

The next Sunday he showed up, and the little girl introduced him to her children's minister, who began a relationship with him. Soon the Muslim student gave his life to Christ, and then he led four of his Muslim friends to Christ.

One long-haired, rough-looking biker showed up at the church the Sunday after Christmas, found Jon Weece, gave him a big hug, and said, "I just had to come meet the preacher who cancelled Christmas!"

The two of them started talking, and eventually the man said, "You know what? I just really need Jesus." They kept talking, and finally the man said, "I want Jesus in my life right now." They prayed together, and that night the man came back to the church and Jon baptized him. Afterward, as they were walking out of the auditorium, the biker looked back in and said, "Jon, I'm going to fill a whole row of this church with my buddies. I have a lot of buddies who need Jesus." In the three years since, this biker has led nineteen of his friends to Christ, and together they fill up two rows of the sanctuary.

You know what's funny? Since Southland is a very high-profile, visible church, the week of Christmas it was named in several news stories as a church that would not have services on Christmas. And Jon Weece received twenty thousand emails from outraged Christians from all over the country.

Why?

Well, maybe it's because a lot of Christians have some small misunderstandings that lead to massive confusion.

And maybe that's a tragedy.

What if you and I were different?

What if we got subversive? What if we went against the grain? What if, by the mere example of how we live our lives, we helped to correct people's misunderstandings? What if we gave up our right to be served and instead lived to serve? What if we redefined greatness? What if we viewed church not as something that brings in people from the community for services but as people who go out into the community to serve?

What might happen?

Maybe we'd develop some shiny heinies?

Maybe we'd radically alter the misunderstandings people *outside* the church have that we're judgmental, selfish, and isolated? Maybe they'd come to understand, through our example, who Jesus is—that he's loving, and a healer, and a grace-giver?

Maybe we'd start a revolution.

It's Time to Talk Guerrilla

1. Who is the most servant-hearted person you know? What do you think makes them such a servant?
2. Read Mark 9:33–35. These friends of Jesus had been with him quite a long time, so why do you think they were still arguing about who was the greatest?
3. What do you think Jesus meant when he said that to be first you must be last? Give some examples of how that could play out in your everyday life.
4. What do you think Jesus meant when he said that to be first you must be servant of all?

5. Do you think there are exceptions? Are there times when a Christian doesn't have to serve or can be served? When and why?

6. Oswald Chambers has written, "[Jesus's] idea is that we serve Him by being the servants of other men. . . . He says that in His Kingdom he that is greatest shall be the servant of all. The real test of the saint is not preaching the gospel, but washing disciples' feet, that is, doing the things that do not count in the actual estimate of men but count everything in the estimate of God."[1] What do you think makes it so difficult to focus on the "estimate" of God and ignore the "estimate" of men?

7. Let's imagine that everyone in your church started believing that true greatness is marked by serving and that the church is people who go out into the community to serve. What kind of impact do you think it would have on the lives of people in your church? And what kind of impact do you think it would have on the lives of people who live around but don't attend your church or any other?

It's Time to Get Guerrilla

What Southland church did was somewhat controversial because the church cancelled its Sunday services (and on Christmas Day!) to go out and serve the community. But this doesn't have to happen on Christmas Day, or even on a Sunday.

Obviously, the goal is to have Christians serving in the community all the time. But perhaps it would be a great kick start for the people in your church if you had one big day where everyone went out and served the community. Maybe that would help you and the people in your church to see the power and greatness of serving.

So why not? Why not have your church do that? And why don't you lead it?

Talk to someone in leadership at your church (try not to sound nuts when you share this idea) about why you think it would be great and how you're willing to coordinate the great day of serving. Get their permission to set a day and promote it to the church.

Then get a team together to help you come up with ideas for serving your community. Plenty of websites list these ideas (such as http://www.helpothers.org/ideas.php and http://www.actsofkindness.org/community#here).

Have your team work through what will be needed for each service opportunity you'll provide.

On the day of serving, have people videotape some of what happens to show in church later, so people who don't participate can see what they missed.

After the day of serving, create a chance to celebrate and share stories of what happened.

For more assignments and ideas, and to learn about and become a part of the Guerrilla Lover movement, go to www.guerrillalovers.com.

COVERT CELLS

Want to really live the Christian life?
  Want to impact the world through guerrilla love?
  Then you must *stop* living in community!

♥

In some African people groups, boys are raised by their mothers until they turn thirteen. Up until that point they live in community with other kids their age doing, well, whatever it is African boys in these people groups do. (Yes, I could conduct research and explain exactly what they do, but I am currently sitting in a hotel room in Poland with very slow Internet access. It's the middle of the night and I'm pretty tired, so I refuse to do the research and instead will guess.)

So, up until that point they live in community with the other kids their age . . . running through the jungle, and fishing, and . . . playing badminton.

But (and this next part is for real) at some point each year the men from the tribe come in under the cover of night and "kidnap" all the boys who are turning thirteen that year. They blindfold them, beat them up some, and take them out to the wilderness. Once there they circumcise the boys (happy birthday!), and then they leave them to fend for themselves for about six months.

This group of boys will start out disoriented and very individualistic, only thinking of themselves. But soon they bond. But their bonding goes beyond their previous friendships; it is now a matter of survival. They have to protect themselves from wild beasts. They work in collaboration to find food and water. Soon they become a tight unit with an unbreakable connection.

An anthropologist named Victor Turner calls this kind of bond *communitas*.[1] Communitas happens in situations where individuals are driven to bond through a common experience of ordeal, humbling, transition, and marginalization. It involves intense feelings of social togetherness and belonging brought about by having to rely on each other in order to survive.

Victor Turner points out that there is a significant contrast between community and communitas. In community people bond, but the reason they're together is self-interest. It's "community for me," not "me for the community," as it is with communitas.

In community people may (or may not) have a purpose. Perhaps they read a book a month together, or share recipes, or write fan mail to boy bands. But in communitas people share a mission that puts them on a life-altering adventure.[2]

Have you ever experienced communitas? For many of us who live in America, one of our first tastes of the transition from community to communitas happened on September 11, 2001. On September 10 we felt secure; on September 11 we felt threatened. On September 10 we lived on a common street as neighbors; on September 11 we had a common enemy. On September 10 we were proud to be Americans; on September 11 we were ready to fight together. On September 10 we may have gotten into debates about things that divide us; on September 11 we were more likely to be crying or praying together.

For all of us, it was personal. But for most of us, it wasn't *up close and personal*, so we didn't fully experience communitas. But picture what it must have been like for someone who lived in New York City on September 11. Better yet, picture what it must have been like for a police officer or fireman or rescue worker who lived in New York City on September 11. Imagine what that day and the days that followed were like for him and his coworkers. *That's* communitas.

♥

So do you want to really live the Christian life? Do you want to impact the world through guerrilla love?

Then you must stop living in community.

One of the biggest problems for Christians is that we live in community, and we'll never really live or change the world until we stop.

Seriously.

Think about your experience of community in the Christian life. It might be the church you belong to and its monthly fellowship meals. Or the Sunday school class you attend. Or the small group that meets in your living room weekly. Or perhaps it's your youth group, or the one you belonged to years ago.

That experience of community—what did it involve? What were the main components?

(I'm being serious: I really want you to think about your experience of community in the Christian life and what components were involved.)

(Did you do it yet?)

(There's no point reading on until you have, so just do it.)

Okay, that experience of community—eating jello with fruit hiding in the middle, discussing what the unpardonable sin might be and that dress the pastor's wife was wearing the other day, playing charades, talking about whether we should do the bake sale again this year, praying for Aunt Iris's arthritis—where do you see anything like that in the Bible? Ummmm . . . nowhere.

My guess is that if you're like most Christians, you've been experiencing community, but God meant for us to live in communitas. In community we see relational connectedness as a nice benefit for us to enjoy when it's convenient. In communitas we see our relational connectedness as necessary for us to survive and thrive. In community our purpose for bonding is to huddle and cuddle. In communitas our purpose for bonding is to have a life-altering adventure we can engage in together.

We've been experiencing community, but we don't see anything like that in the Bible.

Think about Jesus and his first followers. Did he call this group together and say, "Okay guys, now listen. We're gonna huddle . . . and we're gonna cuddle! We'll get together and eat snacks and play games and read the Bible and share prayer requests and have retreats and maybe even have a knitting club! It's gonna be great. Now I want to make it clear that you only have to show up if it's convenient for you . . ."

No, he said, "I want you to follow me, but understand this: if you follow me, it's gonna require everything you have. It will be a life of self-sacrifice. You'll have to put the needs of this group above your own, whether you like it or not. And the mission is paramount. We are starting a revolution to try to convince everyone that a life of loving God and loving people is the best way to live, and that mission must come first in your life. Engaging in this mission is going to get me killed, and it very well may get you killed. So do you want to be a part of this group or not?"

Jesus called people to communitas (to a life-altering adventure we can engage in together), not to community (huddle-and-cuddle Christianity).

The same was true with the earliest Christians. In the book of Acts we find the stories of how they engaged in and spread the revolution. And what we see in Acts is not one of the leaders giving a pep talk: "We're gonna huddle! And we're gonna cuddle! We hope our living in community benefits you, and if not . . . feel free to back out anytime. That's really not an issue. We'll just be glad you came." No, we see this: "All the believers were one in heart and mind. No one claimed that any of his possessions was his own, but they shared everything they had. With great power the apostles continued to testify to the resurrection of the Lord Jesus, and much grace was upon them all. There were no needy persons among them. For from time to time those who owned lands or houses sold them, brought the money from the sales and put it at the apostles' feet, and it was distributed to anyone as he had need."[3]

We see people in the group getting killed for belonging to the group. We see this group causing riots. It's crazy! These people bond deeply, and they take on the world together. And during this time the number of Christians grows by thousands and thousands. Why did it thrive rather than just survive? Because God has called us to communitas, to an adventure we can engage in together, not to community, just huddle-and-cuddle Christianity.

But somewhere along the way *something changed*, and if we want to really live, and if we want to change the world, we must stop living in community.

I've been giving this quite a bit of thought: *why* did things change? I'm still not sure, but my guess is that the reason Christians started doing community instead of communitas is that it felt safer. Communitas seems more dangerous.

What's ironic is that just the opposite is true.

The most dangerous thing for us is to play it safe. When we live for self, arranging our lives so we achieve maximum enjoyment and nothing infringes on our comfort, we die inside.

I'm not denying that Christians need each other, that we need fellowship, or that we need people who share our faith. But we don't need each other so we can stay isolated and insulated from the rest of the world. We need each other so that together we can engage the rest of the world, love the rest of the world, take on challenges together, and maybe even die together. And if we're not willing to do that, then we *will* slowly die together. Rather than thrive, our faith will, at best, survive. Over time it will become boring and brittle and probably even disintegrate.

Playing it safe is the most dangerous way for us to live.

And not only is it dangerous for us, it's also dangerous for *others*, because when we live our lives in community instead of communitas, we miss our purpose, which is *them*.

Think about it this way: Picture, again, being that rescue worker who lived in New York City on September 11, 2001. And let's say that on the morning of September 13 your boss called. "Are you okay?" he asks.

"Yes," you tell him. "We're all fine."

"Listen carefully." His voice is urgent. "Experts are telling us that there are probably people buried alive in the rubble of the World Trade Center buildings. Some of those people still have a chance at life if we find them soon enough. So we're getting everyone together and we're gonna go dig. Can you come right away? And call your unit and have them meet you there."

There's an awkward silence. "Hello, did you hear me?" your boss asks.

"Yeah," you reply. "The problem is that me and the boys already have plans today. We've got a big card game planned. Kind of a tournament we set up. And Jonesey said he would make some of his famous three-layer-dip. Sorry, but we're not going to be able to make it."

Or picture your reply being, "Wait a second. We can't go down there! Don't you remember? Today is the day we're going to have a discussion group on how to save people in the event of an emergency. You want us to skip *that*?"

You can't picture that, can you? The reason you can't is because it's absurd. Teams of rescue workers aren't meant to hang out and play games; they're meant to save people. And they don't sit around discussing how to save people when they have an opportunity to actually save people.

And most of all you can't picture that because lives are at stake. No one whose purpose is to save lives would ignore dying people just so they could experience something nice for themselves.

But how close is that to a description of your experience of Christian community?

Perhaps you've been playing it safe, never realizing that it's the most dangerous way for you to live, not only for you but also for them.

♥

So what should you do about this? Well, you might want to stop huddling and cuddling. You may want to stop living in community and start living in communitas.

Let me share an extreme example, and we'll move backward from there.

I have a friend named Gregg. He has an extra *g* in his name, and he's a pastor, but he's still a very normal guy. He loves baseball and wears a St. Louis Cardinals hat most of the time, and we first connected because he heard me singing a Jimmy Eat World song to myself, and he likes Jimmy Eat World.

Gregg is a normal guy who lives with his wife, his toddler-age daughter, and a cat, plus two physical therapists, a registered nurse, a lawyer, an I.T. guru, a former Marine, a photographer, a business manager, a multilingual Head Start teacher, and two more children. Yes, you read that right; in *one* house there are *fourteen* people and a cat. So why does Gregg live with so many people? Is it by necessity? No, it's by *choice*.

These five couples met at a church and after much discussion decided to buy a house and move in together. And as if it wasn't crazy enough for fourteen people to share one house, the house they share is in a poverty-stricken inner city. So why do they live in such a bad neighborhood? Is it by necessity? No, it's by *choice*.

This group of people chose to live together in an awful area so that they could change that area and reach out to the people who live there. They are fighting for the poor through participating in town hall meetings and local politics. They purchase goods from local merchants in an attempt to help the failing local economy. Together they have bought a building where they are going to open a café to help generate commerce in their town. They will also use this café to build relationships with local people, hoping to show them the love of God.

Does smooshing five families into a crowded house serve their own interests? Well, obviously not. Does living in a down-and-out rough neighborhood make them feel safe? Well, no, it makes them feel like they're in danger.

But more importantly, it makes them feel dangerous. They are primed to do something dramatic for God, and it's because they stopped huddling, stopped cuddling, and instead have a mission they're engaging in together.

Could you move in with a bunch of families in a poverty-stricken inner-city area? Possibly so.

But if not, what *could you do* to point the community you experience with other Christians outward?

Maybe your small group or Sunday school class could adopt a mission. Why not find something you could do together twice a month—tutor underprivileged kids, start a support group for homeless people, or participate in a Big Brother program? Or what if instead of meeting every week in a living room to huddle and cuddle, you take one of those gatherings each month to get out and serve the community?

Or perhaps you could talk to the leadership in your church about making this a congregation-wide initiative. What if you conducted a community needs assessment to find out what's missing in your area? And what if, once you discovered it, your church developed a strategy to meet that need? What if your church became known not for what happens in the church building on Sunday morning but for what happens out in the community the rest of the week?

That's what you really want. That's what I really want. We want communitas. And we don't need to live in the African bush, we don't need a national tragedy, we don't need a hurricane to hit—no, everything we need we already have. Because God has given us a vision: he wants to use us to bring a revolution; he wants us to bond together and to love the world in such a way that we turn the thing upside down. God has called us to action, to serve in our community and around the globe. God has called us not to huddle and cuddle, not to small group Bible studies, but to covert cells that engage in an adventure together.

Want to really live the Christian life?

Want to impact the world through guerrilla love?

Then stop living in community and start living out communitas.

It's Time to Talk Guerrilla

1. Don't talk this one through alone—get together with some friends, preferably people with whom you live in Christian community.

2. Can you think of a movie that portrays individuals who are living for themselves and are completely bored with their lives, but then engage together on some kind of mission which changes everything for them? Examples would include *City Slickers* or *Thelma and Louise*.
3. What do you think it was about engaging in a mission that changed their lives?
4. Have you ever experienced joining together with a group of people for a selfless, outward-focused mission and having it really impact your life?
5. Read Acts 2:42–47 and Acts 4:32–37. Thinking through the experience of togetherness these early Christians had and what you're currently experiencing with the Christians you're closest to, what do you share in common with them?
6. Where is your experience of togetherness very different from theirs?
7. Notice in Acts 2:47 that the result of them living their lives together was people from the outside coming in. Their "fellowship" was not a fortress from the world but rather an open door to the world. How often do you see new people coming into your fellowship?
8. If you don't see new people coming in, why do you think that is? What can you do to change it? And what *will* you do to change it?

It's Time to Get Guerrilla

Invite the people you share life with to a meal at your home. But tell them they have homework to do before they arrive. Everyone must come with a list of ideas. All the ideas must center on how you, as a group, could point your community outward and do something to serve others. Tell them that no idea is too crazy. In fact, encourage them to come with some crazy ideas that probably won't be acceptable to others.

Here are some possibilities to get you started. What if your group: (1) all moved to a foreign country to serve and bring the gospel to the people there, (2) all moved to a new town and together started a new church, (3) all moved to the most downtrodden area in your town and tried to infuse that neighborhood with life, or (4) adopted a grammar school in a poor neighborhood, serving it in every way you can?

When you are together, talk through the questions in the "It's Time to Talk Guerrilla" section for this chapter and then the list of ideas people brought to the meal. For each idea, ask the question, "Is this something God is calling us to do?" Let that be your deciding question, not a list of pros and cons and fears people have.

For each idea, picture what it could look like if you actually did it. Make it a group visualization exercise. If God blessed it in a way only he can, what might happen?

Before you leave, pick an option or two and commit to *at least* giving them serious prayer and further discussion. Choosing something you will actually do would be even better, but if it's a huge step (i.e., moving to another country), it may take more than one meeting to make that decision.

For more assignments and ideas, and to learn about and become a part of the Guerrilla Lover movement, go to www .guerrillalovers.com.

GAS MOLECULES

T. E. Lawrence, better known as "Lawrence of Arabia," wrote an article for the *Encyclopedia Britannica* on guerrilla warfare tactics. In it he compared guerrilla fighters to a gas. The fighters disperse randomly in the area of operations, occupying a very small space in that area, just as gas molecules occupy a small space in a container. The fighters may coalesce into groups for tactical purposes, but their general state is dispersed. Lawrence also proposed never meeting the enemy, so that their soldiers would have nothing to shoot at.

As guerrilla lovers we too must separate, for our impact comes not when we are gathered but when we are dispersed.

However, being a guerrilla lover differs from being a guerrilla fighter in some vital ways. First, we have no enemies. We don't fight an enemy; we love people who have not yet discovered what we have found. And second, to do so, we must meet them. Our goal is to forge relationships with people who are far from God and help them to come close to and forge relationships with God.

We disperse like gas molecules. But we meet with, we get close to, we build relationships, we love—because ultimately our goal is for everyone to have a relationship with God through Jesus.

♥

Shelly Hollis is a young Jesus-follower who took seriously this idea of dispersing. In fact, she dispersed to Haiti. She felt like God was calling her to be a missionary in Haiti, so she went. She moved there to share God's love with people and help them to know Jesus.

One day Shelly stumbled across an elderly woman who hadn't been cared for in days. Her name was Granka. When Shelly found her she was dehydrated and near death. What began as a fever had turned deadly simply because of neglect. No one was taking care of her. Shelly found Granka soaked in urine and sweat, lying on a little bed. Her family had come in the night before and taken all of her personal belongings and divided them up amongst themselves. They even went so far as to put a coffin beside her bed. Their message was clear: they weren't hoping she'd get better any time soon. They left her for dead. Shelly's heart broke when she found Granka. She stayed with Granka through the night. She cleaned her up, fed her, prayed for her. This went on for several days, but to no avail. Finally Granka died.

The next morning Shelly was sitting at a picnic table outside the school where she worked, head in her hands, exhausted, worn out. When a friend sat down next to her, Shelly began to weep. They sat there for several minutes until finally, trying to gain her composure, she blurted out, "I didn't tell her. I didn't get to tell her about Jesus."

♥

Do you agree with Shelly's evaluation of what happened? Should she have been satisfied with caring for this dying woman, or was she right that because she didn't tell her about Jesus, her guerrilla love was somehow incomplete? Is it enough to love, to care for needs, to feed the hungry, to clothe the naked?

I don't think so.

All of that *is* critical (I mean, I'm sitting here writing an entire book about it!), we are called by God to do it, and it's almost always the best way to start, but ultimately we need to tell people about Jesus.

Why?

Well, in part because a relationship with God is the best thing life has to offer. Nothing else compares to it. It is *the* most important thing. I love the story Jesus told about this dude who is really into pearls.[1] In fact, he travels all around buying up pearls. He wants nothing more than to have a huge collection of pearls. Then one day he discovers the ultimate pearl. Even with all his experience going after pearls, he had no idea such a pearl could exist. Suddenly all his pursuits seem silly. His collection of pearls pales in comparison. In fact, he immediately loses his desire for any other pearls. He only wants this one. It's that good. He has to sell all his other pearls and everything he has to be able to afford to buy this pearl, but he doesn't even blink. He gladly gives up everything because he knows nothing else could compare to having this pearl.

Jesus wasn't really telling a story about pearls. His point was that the ultimate goal of life is having a relationship with God. That nothing else compares to it. That we shouldn't hesitate to give up everything for it, and if we had to, it would still be the greatest bargain imaginable.

We need to know that and stay focused on it.

But we don't. We get distracted by so many other things. Some selfish, some not.

Last Sunday a guy came up to me after our church service and said, "This was amazing! I want this in my life! I just signed up to get called about baptism." I congratulated him and told him that was great and to be expecting a call the next day. But why didn't I invite him to come over to my house to talk about it? Why didn't I take him out to lunch? Well, I had other plans. I had other things I had to do.

Seriously?

I've lost my focus. Because *nothing* compares to having a relationship with God and helping someone else to have that relationship.

We can't let anything distract us from that.

We need to remember that this is why we love, why we serve—because ultimately we hope that people will see Jesus in us and want to know Jesus for themselves.

Sometimes we get distracted by the act of serving itself. We need to serve, but serving is not the end. It's a path to help people to the ultimate good.

That doesn't mean we're serving with an ulterior motive. Imagine a loving mother trying to get a spoonful of needed medicine into her child's mouth. Is getting the medicine into the mouth the ultimate goal? Of course not. What she wants to do is bring wellness to her child. So is she giving him the medicine with an ulterior motive? No, it's with an *ultimate* motive, a *superior* motive. A motive that is intrinsically connected and far more important. And we serve for all kinds of reasons, but the ultimate and superior motive is for people to know Jesus and experience a life-changing relationship with God.

Yes, we want to protect the environment, eradicate poverty, end the AIDS epidemic in Africa, and provide the homeless with places to live. And make no mistake, all of that *is* important. But it doesn't compare to helping people know Jesus. If we serve people but we're not trying to help them find that relationship with God, we've missed it. And they will miss out.

If we send people off well fed and well clothed to life and eternity without Jesus, what have we really done? Will they thank us?

Ultimately what everyone needs, and what everyone wants—whether they realize it or not—is a relationship with

God. A real, vibrant, deep, authentic, intimate relationship with God.

Nothing else compares to the treasure of having that relationship with God.

I think about how much I love my wife and love being with her. If you asked me if I would rather live in a palatial mansion by myself or be homeless with Jen . . . well, I'd rather be homeless with Jen.

It's like that.

God is a greater treasure than anything else this life has to offer. Now that I've experienced a relationship with God, real intimacy with God, I'd rather have cancer and AIDS and poverty *with* God than perfect health and success and abundant riches *without* God.

So many of us want all this other stuff in life, but that only shows that we haven't yet fully experienced a relationship with God. We also want all this other stuff for people, for them to be taken care of and not suffer. All of that is good, but if we want that for them and aren't ultimately trying to help them have a relationship with God, that only shows that we haven't yet fully experienced a relationship with God.

Because nothing compares to it. It's a treasure worth pursuing with our whole lives. It's worth giving everything we have to get. And it's what we should want for everyone.

Now, this doesn't diminish guerrilla love. It doesn't take away from anything we've talked about. We need to serve and forgive and throw parties and share our resources and touch the sick, but our ultimate hope in doing so is that people will see Jesus in us. I'm convinced that what the world is looking for is not a life-changing message but a life that's been changed by the message. When they see the beauty of our lives and feel the love we have, that's what gets their attention.

The world has had too much in-your-face evangelism. I just read an article in my local newspaper entitled, "Oceanfront Preachers Deliver Message with an Attitude." It's about some guys who stand on corners down by the beach yelling, "God will judge you!" at pedestrians. One of the street preachers is quoted as saying, "Our ministry is a shock-and-awe of evangelism, and we're into the face of the sinner with the sins." What's amazing is that this guy freely admits that his method is not effective and that they don't see people coming to Christ. But for some reason I can't fathom, he continues to do it. His street preaching has led to his being assaulted and spit on, and one lady even smacked him with a bag of rotten fish (which raises the question, who carries around bags of rotten fish?).[2]

This guy and people like him aren't doing anyone any good. The way of Jesus is the way of love. We're called to love, to serve, to meet needs. And if we never see people come to Christ, well, at least we did some good. At least we were known for our love. At least we made our world a little bit better place.

And that's good stuff.

But it's obviously not the ideal.

Because it doesn't compare to experiencing a relationship with God.

Everyone needs that. Everyone needs Jesus. And we should be willing to do anything we can to get them to him.

Shelly Hollis sat at that picnic table heartbroken that she hadn't been able to tell the dying woman about Jesus. And she prayed. She prayed that God would put another elderly woman into her path with whom she could share her faith. She felt confident that God was going to do that for her. She committed to do that for him.

Very late one night not long after, Shelly was leaving church when a Haitian man jumped out from between two houses, grabbed her by her shirt, and swung her into a nearby wall. Shelly hit the ground disoriented, her shoulder dislocated. This guy jumped on top of her and began to remove her clothes. She fought with everything inside of her. Biting him and hitting him with her flashlight, she managed to get away. She ran down the street screaming for help. Shelly opened the door of the first house she came to, ran in, and collapsed onto the floor in shock. In the back of that house the elderly Haitian woman who lived there, a woman named Fatalia, woke up, ran to see what all the commotion was, lit a candle, and saw Shelly lying on the ground. Fatalia called for help and cleaned Shelly's wounds.

The next morning Shelly called her family to let them know what had happened. Her dad said, "Come home! That's enough. Just come home now. Today!"

And who can blame him? If someone tried to rape your daughter, you'd say the same thing. And who'd blame Shelly if she took his advice? Maybe God had called her to Haiti, maybe not, but she had gone. She had been faithful to him. Certainly it was time to call it quits and go home.

But Shelly told her father, "I prayed that God would give me another elderly woman to share my faith with, and this is that opportunity." So Shelly stayed on. She went to Fatalia's house and told her about Jesus. And not too much later, Shelly and Fatalia stood on a beach, then walked into the ocean, and Shelly baptized Fatalia.

Fast-forward two years. Shelly was walking to her church in Haiti on a Sunday morning when she looked up and saw the man who'd tried to rape her. His name was Parnal. He had spent the last two years in jail because of what he had done to Shelly. She did not know he had just gotten out, and she says that her heart started racing with fear as their eyes met. She cried the entire way to church and walked as fast as she could.

"Then I put my hand on the door to the church, and I just couldn't open it," she later said.

She felt like God was calling her to go and share her faith, to share his love, with that man Parnal.

Now that's just plain nuts.

Even if that was God speaking to her, certainly it would be understandable to ignore him. The man she felt like she was supposed to talk with was the man who had tried to rape her. Why would she try to help him? Wouldn't it be dangerous if they were alone when she found him?

But Shelly turned around and raced back down the street, looking for this man. When she finally found him, she hugged him and said, "I have forgiven you, and I want you to come to church with me so you can understand why."

A few minutes later they walked hand-in-hand into the church together.

See the power of dispersing? Shelly could have easily ignored God's call to go to and stay in Haiti. I mean, who wants to live in Haiti? But if Shelly didn't disperse to Haiti, Fatalia and Parnal's lives might never have been touched. But because the small, young gas molecule that is Shelly Hollis came floating into Haiti, their lives were changed forever.

Maybe you've been coalescing in a small container with a bunch of other gas molecules, but you were meant to be dispersed. Only when you separate can you have your intended and greatest impact.

So what are you waiting for, gas molecules? It's time to disperse.

It's time to give your Christian friends a long hug, tell 'em you'll see them on Sunday, and invite some friends from work over for a party. It's time to let your church buddies know you'll keep up on Facebook and get face-to-face with your neighbors. It's time to quit one of your church activities so you can free up some time to hang out at the softball field or in a bar, so that those people might end up in church.

We disperse like gas molecules. We meet with, get close to, build relationships, and love because ultimately our goal is for everyone to have a relationship with God through Jesus.

So go.

(Now.)

(Stop reading, put the book down, and go.)

(Seriously. I'm not kidding. Put the stupid book down and go.)

It's Time to Talk Guerrilla

1. Think about how you came to faith. Who helped you to get there? What was it about that person that impacted you? What did that person do to help you?
2. Why do you think so few Christians share their faith? More personally, why do you struggle to share your faith?
3. Think through all the excuses you have for not sharing your faith. (Maybe: "I'm not good at telling people about Jesus," or "I'm not a good enough example," or "I wouldn't be able to answer their questions.") Do you notice that all your excuses focus on *you*?
4. Why does that matter? Well, because *you* are not the one responsible for changing people's hearts; *God is*. Your responsibility isn't to convince people or get them to accept Jesus; it's to love people and to look for opportunities to (gently) share with them who Jesus is and what he's done in your life.
5. How might your feelings about sharing your faith change if you really understood that God is the only one who can convince and change a person?
6. Read 1 Peter 3:15–16. Notice the assumption that people will ask you about your faith. What about your life might force people to ask questions?
7. Notice also that it mentions your "good behavior." Do you think that could be referring to guerrilla love kind of acts? What about guerrilla lovefare might lead people to ask questions?
8. Why do you think the verse puts an emphasis on speaking with "gentleness and respect"? How can gentleness and respect help people to really hear the message, and

how can a lack thereof keep people from really hearing the message?

9. When you think about how Christians (in general) talk to people about Jesus, do you think of "gentleness and respect"? If not, how could you change that image?

It's Time to Get Guerrilla

Maybe part of the reason we struggle with sharing Jesus is because *so* many people need Jesus. It's rather intimidating, and we think, "What can *I* do?"

So let's narrow the scope of our mission. Many cell phone companies have "Fave Five" kinds of plans where you choose five people you can call for free. Obviously we want everyone to know Jesus, but why don't you choose five people to focus on? Think through your extended family, friends, neighbors, coworkers, acquaintances from school or sports, and so on. Maybe write down everyone you know. Of that list, choose five people you're pretty sure don't have an active relationship with God and don't regularly attend church.

Got your five? Here's what we're going to do with that list:

First, we're going to commit to praying for them daily. If you need reminders, create reminders. Every day we're going to pray that our friends develop a spiritual thirst and an openness to a relationship with God through Jesus.

Second, we're going to serve them. We're going to ambush our five with guerrilla lovefare attacks. It doesn't have to be, and probably shouldn't be, anything weird. Just serve and meet their needs. Let God love your five through you.

Third, we're going to pray and look for strategic opportunities to invite them to church or church events. This assumes that you attend a church that won't turn them off. If you do, disregard this step.

Fourth, we're going to pray and look for strategic opportunities to share our faith with them. This doesn't necessarily mean a full "gospel presentation." It may just be you sharing something God's done in your life recently. It may just be asking some questions about their spiritual views.

Will this eventually lead the person into a relationship with God? Who knows? But that's not your responsibility. Your responsibility is to pray, serve, invite, and share.

For more assignments and ideas, and to learn about and become a part of the Guerrilla Lover movement, go to www .guerrillalovers.com.

WORLDWIDE REVOLUTION

It's not about religion; it's about a relationship. It's about a relationship with God that revolutionizes our lives and turns us into revolutionaries. The revolution that's happened inside us starts to seep out, and we begin sharing it with others.

Some of us have only had a religion with God. Others of us have a relationship, but we haven't begun sharing it yet.

But maybe you have heard and responded to the call to start ambushing the people God puts in your path with his love. If so, that's great. But it still doesn't go quite far enough. The revolutionary leader has an even bigger vision for your life. He said, "Go into all the world and preach the good news to all creation,"[1] and, "you will be my witnesses in Jerusalem, and in all Judea and Samaria, and to the ends of the earth."[2]

Jesus's love isn't limited to you, your family, or your cul-de-sac. He loves the world, and you are part of his plan for reaching the world. He wants you to be an *international* guerrilla lover.

Personally, I knew all that, but I had some excuses that I thought might mean I could ignore it.

One, I had never really traveled outside America. Well, I think I was conceived in Puerto Rico, but I'm not sure if that counts. (Somewhere out there a sperm and an egg are smoking cigarettes, smiling, and saying, "Oh yeah, baby, it counted.")

I also couldn't speak a foreign language. This was not for lack of trying. I took Spanish in high school. Well, I took Spanish until I was barred from the class. I wasn't exactly the best kid back then, and some teachers knew how to handle me, while others didn't. Mr. Fuentes, our Spanish teacher, definitely did *not* know how to handle me. I don't know why he considered me a problem. It wasn't like I was bringing weapons to school (well, maybe one or two) or getting in fights (okay, a few) or selling drugs (well, never in *his* class). What I did was talk a lot. I was *that* guy, the funny guy. Anyway, Mr. Fuentes would periodically go into fits of rage where he would yell at me and my friends, alternating between English and Spanish, which made him sound a lot like Ricky Ricardo on *I Love Lucy*. This made me act even funnier (or more annoying, depending on your perspective). Mr. Fuentes would scream, "You kids, I'm going *fuera de mi cabeza*! I am going *loco por ti*!" And I'd whisper to my friends, "When Mr. Fuentes gets home from the Babalu club, Lucy will have some 'splaining to do!"

Well, one day it was just too much for Mr. Fuentes. As he cursed at us in Spanish (I don't know for sure that he was cursing, but it's a safe assumption), he looked like some veins were about to burst on his forehead and his eyes were going to explode out of their sockets, and something just snapped in his brain. He stared at me and my friends, and then I wasn't sure why, but he started looking around the room. Then I realized—he was searching for a weapon. Unable to find anything lighter than a desk, he picked one up and threw it at us. It bounced toward us and we dove under our desks screaming, "Ricky!" and "Fred, Ethel, save meeeee!" I thought the whole thing was really funny until the next day when the principal informed me I was not allowed to return to Spanish class.

My lack of good study habits, odd sense of humor, and limited time with Mr. Crazy Latino Temper Man left me with only a few Spanish phrases I still remember: "*El sandia esta loco*" (The watermelon is crazy), "*Me tiro en su cuarto de bano*" (I just threw up in your bathroom), and "*Por favor, conseguir la mano de mis pantalones*" (Please get your hand out of my pants).

I didn't figure any of those would help me preach the Good News to all creation.

Still, I knew I was supposed to share God's love with people outside the box of my little neighborhood in America. So when we started a church in Virginia Beach, we decided that someday we would try to reach an unreached people group.

What is an unreached people group, you ask? A "people group" is a group of people who share a common self-identity, language, history, and customs. For those of us living in the melting pot of America, this is a pretty foreign idea, but in many parts of the world two different people groups may live very close to each other, but because of a lack of transportation and communication, they may not even be aware the other group exists, as they simply keep to themselves. Or they may be aware of other groups but ignore them or perhaps just acknowledge them and trade goods with them.

The "unreached" part refers to people groups who have never been touched by the gospel. They have still not even heard the name of Jesus.

We decided to "adopt" one of these unreached people groups and seek to serve and love them and, hopefully, introduce them to Jesus.

We had absolutely no idea how we would do this. We knew virtually nothing about missions, and we knew nothing about unreached people groups. But we started praying that God would lead us to one.

We made that decision in 1998, and by the spring of 2001 God led us to a specific people group.[3] They're unreached because they live in Communist nations in Southeast Asia where telling people about Jesus is illegal. They're also unreached because they live up in the mountains. They're kind of reclusive, so as modern society creeps up the mountain, they move farther up to avoid it. They also generally speak their own language, rather than one of the main languages of their nation.

Don't miss this. The people in the unreached people group we picked live in countries where talking about Jesus is illegal. They reside in mountains that are difficult to navigate. And they speak a language we probably couldn't learn even if we wanted to.

In July of 2001 I stood on a stage in front of our young church and said, "We've been praying about it and talking about it, and today is the day!" (Everyone cheered wildly.) "We are making a commitment to reach this people group!" (Everyone cheered wildly again.) "Now, I must admit; I have never seen a person from this people group." (No wild cheering.) "I can't imagine how we'll ever even meet a person from this people group." (Puzzled looks.) "I don't have a clue how we could possibly reach one of them; I mean, we're not even really allowed into their countries, and we can't speak their language." (Blank stares.) "But . . . we're gonna do it!" (Half-hearted applause, kind of like you'd give the 280-pound guy who enters a marathon, walks the whole way, and collapses in a puddle of sweat 40 yards before the finish line. You know, that applause that says, "You're pretty pathetic, but we feel bad for you, and we sort of appreciate the effort you put into this, though we don't really understand what you're trying to prove here.")

We talked about how, in the Old Testament, when God did something special, people often would build altars to commemorate it. And we proceeded to build an altar together, right on the stage of the high school we were meeting in.

In one sense the whole thing was very cool, though I have to admit, it did feel a bit ridiculous. Like, who are we kidding here? But we knew God commanded us to go into all the world, we wanted to obey him and be international guerrilla lovers, and we had faith that maybe God would help us.

So what about you? You may not have traveled much internationally, and perhaps you don't know a foreign language. But, even still, God has called you to join his *worldwide* revolution. You need to obey him, even if you don't know what to do or how to do it. And who knows? Maybe God will help you.

So what could you do to become an international guerrilla lover? What about sponsoring a child with Compassion International? For about $40 a month you can provide opportunities for education, health, and personal development. And ultimately even more important, the child you sponsor will learn about Jesus in a church-based program. You could do that![4]

Or what about helping someone to start a micro-business? In many parts of the world a person can start a business for $40. Christian organizations like Kiva (www.kiva.org) and I Was Hungry (https://www.heavensfamily.org/iwh/microloan) go into the poorest places in the world and give $40 to individuals. For example, a woman in a village in Africa who has nothing will receive $40 to start a business, and she'll open a little stall in a street market where she'll sell stuff. And from that business she'll be able to build a house for her family and put food on their table every day. All that because of $40! And these organizations take $40 donations from people like you and me. You could do that! You could give someone a business so they can escape poverty and provide for their family.[5]

Or what about getting some foreign soil under your shoes by going on a mission trip? If your church does mission trips, pray about which one you will go on. If you don't feel like God is leading you to one specific trip, just go on any one you can.

Want to get really crazy? Pray about God maybe sending you on a *permanent* mission trip. Perhaps you could start the process by asking God to give you a heart for a country. Ask him to put it on your heart to start praying consistently for one country. Once you start praying for that country, maybe God will push you further and show you how you could become a guerrilla lover to that nation.

Is all of this crazy? Well, yeah, probably. But is that a bad thing? Shouldn't people who believe in and follow Jesus have lives that look a little crazy compared to everyone else's? And it may seem like you wouldn't know what to do and even if you did it wouldn't work, but maybe God will help you.

Maybe. This reminds me of a crazy story from 1 Samuel 14 in the Bible. The Israelites (the people who believe in God) are having problems with their enemies, the Philistines, and they're on the verge of war. The Israelites have been sitting around for a while, not far from the Philistine army. There are about 600 Israelites but thousands of Philistines, so they're too afraid to fight.

Jonathan, who is the son of Israel's King, Saul, asks his friend to go with him closer to the Philistines. We're not told what Jonathan was thinking, but I wonder if perhaps it was, "Man, I can't just sit around here anymore. I've got to do *something*." Some times in life we have to do something. We can't sit anymore, wait anymore, prepare anymore, second-guess anymore, analyze anymore, argue anymore, discuss anymore, study anymore, worry anymore, complain anymore, look over our shoulder anymore, or make excuses anymore. We've just got to move. And that's exactly what Jonathan did.

Interestingly, the Bible says that he didn't tell his father what he was going to do. Why not? Well, his father probably would have said, "No, you're not going. It's crazy. Why would you go over there? Things are fine the way they are."

The same applies to you. If you tell people what you're thinking of doing, you'll very likely get similar comments. "No, you're not going on that mission trip." "It's crazy to help someone in India start a business. You don't even have enough money for yourself." "You want to move to the inner city to be a missionary to the people who live there? No! I mean, why would you go over there? Just stay here." "You're thinking of doing what? Is this because of that book you read? Just stop. Things are fine the way they are."

If we choose to be revolutionaries for God, and maybe especially if we start exploring ways to become international guerrilla lovers, some people are bound to think we're crazy. Unfortunately, many of these people will be Christians. I'm not sure what Bible they're reading, but somehow they think God wants us to play it safe and be comfortable.

He doesn't.

Continuing with the story, Jonathan says to his friend, "Come, let's go over to the outpost of those uncircumcised fellows. Perhaps the LORD will act in our behalf."[6] I have to say I find something hysterical about a guy calling his enemies "those uncircumcised fellows." First, when I'm thinking about my enemies, I don't want to be focused on or even mentioning anything below the waist (if you know what I'm saying). And, second . . . *fellows*? For real? This guy is so bold that he's going into a possible two vs. thousands fight, and he calls them *fellows*? He might as well have said, spear in hand, "Let's have an outing and pay a little visit to our chums, shall we, ol' chap?"

But what I find most intriguing is that Jonathan says, "*Perhaps* the LORD will act in our behalf." You and I won't commit to doing anything unless we're absolutely certain God has "called" us to do it and we've lined up everything so success is basically guaranteed. We eliminate any possibility of failure and therefore any need for faith.

Not so with Jonathan.

He doesn't seem the least bit sure that God is telling him to do it or that it will go well. He just knows he has to do something and, well, perhaps God will help. Maybe.

Now, Jonathan *does* have a strategy. It just happens to be the stupidest strategy ever devised. Check this out. He says, "Come, then; we will cross over toward the men and let them see us. If they say to us, 'Wait there until we come to you,' we will stay where we are and not go up to them. But if they say, 'Come up to us,' we will climb up, because that will be our sign that the LORD has given them into our hands."[7]

Do you ever read the Bible and think, "That makes absolutely no sense!" I read this and think, *Jonathan is an idiot*! I mean, I love how he took initiative. I appreciate how he gathered a team—but his team consists of only one person! And his strategy is to walk up "and let them see us." I'm no General Patton, but I think *not* being seen by your enemy is usually the better approach. From there his strategy is to do whatever the enemy wants him to do. "If they want me to stay, I'll stay. If they want me to come, I'll come. If those fellows would like cheese and crackers, by golly, I'll bring them cheese and crackers!" I mean, seriously, can you imagine the President of the United States calling the leader of a terrorist movement and saying, "Hey, could you tell us what you'd like us to do? Because whatever it is, we'll do it. You call the shots here." That's what Jonathan did!

So what do we learn from Jonathan's example? Well, we learn how to be really dumb, for one thing (and that's always helpful), but the lesson I take from it is about risk. When we decide to take initiative for God, we will take risks. We'd like to eliminate all the unknowns and have a well-developed strategy we can rely on . . . but maybe it's better to just rely on God. Perhaps God works best through foolish people and stupid strategies because those people are forced to look to God rather than their own wisdom, and when they succeed, no one will give them the credit. "Yeah, it was the doofus with the idiotic plan; that's why it worked." No, when bozos with bad strategies succeed, God gets the glory.

So Jonathan and his friend go over, making sure their enemies see them, and the Philistines yell, "Come up to us and we'll bash your brains in!" Jonathan says something like, "Jolly good! These lads have requested our presence at a brain bashing. That means God shall give us triumph in our quest!"

Next we read, "Jonathan climbed up, using his hands and feet."[8] (I'm so glad that detail was included. Without it, I would have pictured Jonathan climbing up using his ears and butt cheeks.) When he gets to the top, guess what he discovers? He didn't need the "perhaps." It wasn't, "Perhaps the Lord will act in our behalf"; it was, "The Lord *will* act in our behalf."

God comes through in a big way as Jonathan and his friend start taking out multiple Philistines, which inspires the other Israelites to join them in the fight, and they have a total God-given victory.

Why? Why did God come through for Jonathan?

Well, I don't know. The Bible doesn't tell us. But I have my suspicions. I think God *loves* it when we know what he's commanded us to do and, rather than make excuses, we take initiative. He loves when we stare our fears in the eye and move forward, taking whatever risks are necessary to obey God.

Earlier I shared how we decided to adopt an unreached people group who live up in the mountains of Communist nations in Southeast Asia—and how we had absolutely no clue how we might be a part of reaching them. All we had was a Jonathan-like faith: "Perhaps the Lord will act on our behalf."

Well, almost immediately some things started happening in one of those countries. We had someone move there to start a chicken farm near a village of our people group. The idea was for him to develop relationships with the people from our people group and give some of them jobs.

Then an entire family from our church moved there, a father and mother and their four kids. They got jobs teaching English as a second language.

Then we started doing short-term trips to that country. Dozens of people from our church would go to help out with the businesses we were involved in, do prayer walks, and serve street kids.

Before long a bunch of people from our people group in that country had heard about Jesus. In fact, several dozen put their faith in and decided to follow him. It was unbelievable!

I started praying, "Okay, God, you're acting on our behalf in that nation, but only forty thousand of our people group are there. Next you need to get us into the neighboring country, where four hundred thousand of our people group live. How will we get in there? Get us into that country, God!" Then one day I got an email from a pastor of a church in Texas who had also adopted an unreached people group in that country.

About ten years before sending me that email, this pastor did one of the dumbest things I've ever heard of. It was very Jonathan-like. He flew to the country, arranged a meeting with a high-up government official, and said, "My church in Texas really cares about your people. Would you allow us to come and serve your people?" Now, understand, he was talking to an atheistic Communist official who leads a country that has been in the news repeatedly for persecuting Christians.

This guy said, "Absolutely not. We don't allow churches to preach sermons and hand out religious literature."

But the pastor replied, "No, we will not preach sermons or hand out religious literature. We want to serve. We want to help. We want to make your nation a better place to live. And we won't talk about Jesus, unless someone asks us why we're serving; then we would have to explain that it's because of our faith in Jesus, because of our relationship with Jesus."

The government official said, "I like you. Let's give this a chance."

So the church started doing community service projects and humanitarian aid, incredible stuff, all over this country. Finally, after ten years, the government asked, "Are there any other churches that would do this?"

Well, I had met this pastor once. I don't know how he remembered me, but he emailed me and asked, "Do you want to go to this country? Your church could serve there."

I replied, "I would be *very* interested, but only if we can serve the people group we adopted. We made a commitment to them; our focus would have to be on them."

He responded, "Sure. Absolutely."

So I went on a trip. And then I planned to go on a second trip with a few other people from my church. On this second trip we hoped to meet with government officials to get approval to do service projects in their country. After years of coordinating everything from Texas, that church now had an employee (named Shane) in the country who helped to coordinate trips and serve as an interpreter. He scheduled our trip. The first day we were to meet with the government officials. The second day we were going up a mountain to see a village where our people group lives.

On the first day we were there, we were about to go into the meeting when I reminded Shane that we wanted to serve our people group. I asked him to tell the government officials this. Shane gave me a weird look. "What are you talking about?"

"You know," I answered him, "we want to serve our specific people group."

"I can't say that to them," Shane says.

"Why?"

Shane explained, "Vince, if I tell them that you only want to serve one people group, that will raise red flags. They won't let you serve."

I started getting mad. "Your pastor told me we could!"

"I'm sorry, Vince," Shane said, "but he was wrong."

We went into the tense meeting with the Communist government officials. We all introduced ourselves and talked for a while, and finally they said, "Okay, yes, you can do service projects in our country."

Shane said, "Great. Thank you. Would you please give them some ideas for projects they can do here for you?"

"Yes," the government official said, "We looked at your itinerary and we saw the village you're planning on visiting tomorrow. This is a people group with many needs. We were wondering, would you be willing to focus all your efforts on that people group?"

Unbelievable!

In 2001 I stood on a stage and said, "I don't know how we'll ever get into these Communist countries; I don't know how we'll be able to serve this people group," and in 2006 a Communist official asked us if we would please come and serve them.

Unbelievable!

We've been doing multiple trips to that nation every year since. We've put in water filtration systems in their village, where people die regularly because of drinking dirty water. We're teaching hygiene and caring for basic health needs. We're teaching them waste management. We're teaching their children English, which will help them get jobs in nearby towns. We've put computers in their schools.

Unbelievable!

And you know what? What God did for Jonathan, and what he did for our church, he could do for you.

So what about you?

Don't you hear the call of God? It's not for someone else. It's for you. Just in case you're having trouble hearing it, I'll share it with you. And in honor of Mr. Fuentes, I'll even tell it to you in Spanish (with translation for my non-bilingual friends). So, here you go:

Puede ser un amante guerrillero internacional! (You can be an international guerrilla lover!)

Viva la Revolución en todo el mundo! (Live the worldwide revolution!)

Por favor, conseguir la mano de mis pantalones! (Please get your hand out of my pants!)

It's Time to Talk Guerrilla

1. What is the best international experience you've ever had?
2. If you could go to one place in the world you've never been, where would it be?
3. Read (or if you're in a group, have different people each read): Psalm 22:27; Psalm 96:3; Matthew 24:14; Matthew 28:19; Mark 16:15; Acts 1:8; Romans 10:14–15; and Revelation 14:6.
4. Why do you think spreading the revolution worldwide is such a big deal to God?
5. Considering those verses, do you think it's okay for a Christian not to have a passport? Why or why not?
6. Have you ever felt God leading you to go to some other country? Did you go? If not, why not? If so, how did it turn out?
7. Has God given you a "burden" for any country or people group? If so, which one, and why do you think it's that one?
8. If God has given you a burden for a country or people group, what will you do about it?

9. If not, you need to know about William Carey. In the late 1700s, William Carey was an ordinary shoemaker who loved God and people. He would get together regularly with a few other guys, and together they would pray for the nations. They would pray for each country, that God would bring his message of life and hope through Jesus to the people who lived there. After doing that for a while, Carey felt drawn to India. He had no idea why, but he packed his bags and moved his family there. Carey eventually became one of the most effective and famous missionaries in history.

10. Why don't you start getting together with some friends to pray for the nations? And why don't you ask God to draw your heart to one of them? And if he does, why don't you do something about it?

It's Time to Get Guerrilla

As a nine-year-old kid in Phoenix, Arizona, Austin Gutwein saw a video about the AIDS epidemic in Africa and the tens of thousands of kids who have been left orphans because of it. As a nine-year-old I wouldn't have given it a second thought. Even today I tend to not take action when I hear of problems around the world. But Austin is different. He decided he had to do something about it. He called a charity group to ask how he could help. The man he spoke to asked Austin his favorite sport. "Basketball," he said. The man responded, "Figure out a way to use basketball to make money to help the orphans in Africa." Because of that conversation Austin launched Hoops of Hope (check out www.hoopsofhope.org or go to www.youtube.com and type "Hoops of Hope" in the search box to check out some news stories), a nonprofit organization that raises awareness and funds by challenging kids all over the world to shoot free throws and raise money for kids in Africa, specifically in Zambia. The first year Austin raised $3,000. He's now raising a couple hundred thousand dollars a year!

What problems around the globe has God made you aware of? And how can you take action? Perhaps you could use something you have or something you love (maybe even something as simple as your favorite sport) to do something to help solve the problem.

So what is the problem?

How can you take action?

What do you have or love that you could use?

How could you raise money?

What could you do if you got out your passport and went to where the problem is?

For more assignments and ideas, and to learn about and become a part of the Guerrilla Lover movement, go to www .guerrillalovers.com.

part 3

EXCUSES

REVOLUTIONARY RISK

Julio Diaz is a thirty-one-year-old social worker who often gets off the subway one stop before his station in the Bronx so he can eat at his favorite diner. One night he stepped off the No. 6 train and began walking toward the stairs when a teenage boy approached, flashed a knife, and demanded all of his money. Diaz was startled, pulled out his wallet, handed it over, and said, "Here you go."

I want to pause the story there and ask you a question: What would *you* do in that situation? Hand over your wallet? Hurry away after the boy left? Feel violated? Tell the police? Call your friends to tell them how bad your life is and ask why these things always seem to happen to you?

What would you do?

Okay, let's hit play: Diaz handed over his wallet and said, "Here you go." The teenager began walking away, but Diaz called after him.

"Hey, wait a minute. You forgot something," Diaz said. "If you're going to be robbing people for the rest of the night, you might as well take my coat to keep you warm."

Diaz began taking off his coat. The boy gave him a confused look and asked, "Why are you doing this?"

"If you're willing to risk your freedom for a few dollars," Diaz answered, "then I guess you must really need the money."[1]

Let's pause the story again, because I need to ask you: If you got mugged a thousand times, would it ever occur to you to do something like that? And even if did occur to you, would you do it? My guess is that you wouldn't, even if it appealed to you as the guerrilla lover thing to do. And the reason you wouldn't is because it would feel too risky.

♥

We've talked about God's call for you to be a guerrilla lover, and I bet you have some ideas of how you could start living guerrilla. Perhaps you've even heard the whisper of God, calling you to some loving action.

I want to take these last few chapters to talk you out onto the ledge.

I want you to jump.

But I'm guessing a few things are holding you back. So let's take them on, one at a time. In this chapter: risk.

Maybe you're thinking about finally forgiving your friend, but what if you do and he betrays you again?

Or what if simplifying your life and sharing more of what you have means you have to continue driving your car that keeps breaking down, or maybe you won't end up with enough saved for retirement?

Or you're considering volunteering at an AIDS hospice, but what if you can't take watching people die slowly, or if it takes so much of your time that you have none left for yourself?

To go guerrilla almost always requires at least a little risk.

So how do you get yourself to risk?

♥

Willingness to risk is based on potential return.[2]

Jesus had some very sobering teachings on counting the cost. When we are about to make a decision, we need to think through what it will cost us. That is critical. But we also have to *count the reward*, because our willingness to risk is based on potential return.

For instance, let's say your house is on fire and you run out screaming like Jamie Lee Curtis in the first *Halloween* movie. Then suddenly you realize . . . your goldfish is still inside! Would you run back into a flaming house to save your goldfish? Of course not. But what about this scenario? Your house is on fire, you get out, but then suddenly you realize . . . your child is still inside! Would you go back in for your kid? Of course you would. Why? Because the return is worth the risk.

Let's look at this in a different way: Let's say I propose a coin flip, and you can call it in the air. You bet $100 and will get $10 if you call it correctly, but if you lose, I get your $100. You're not taking that bet. But what if the deal is that you put up $100 and will get one million dollars if you call it correctly, but if you lose, I get your $100? Would you do that? Of course! Even if you're totally opposed to gambling, you'd change your theology to take that bet!

See how this principle plays out? Willingness to risk is based on potential return. The problem is that when we face a risk, we tend to count the cost but not the reward. We ignore the potential return. We need to count the reward. We need to see the good that often comes out of risk.

In fact, my guess is that almost all the good things in your life are the result of risk. As I look at my own life, I realize that most of the good things in it are the byproduct of risk. Asking my *wife* to marry me was a risk. What if she said no? Or what if she said yes, but we weren't really meant for each other? My *kids* are the result of risk. We could have been held back by fear. What if we couldn't afford them? What if we were bad parents? Becoming a *pastor* was the result of a huge risk. I left law school (and a full scholarship) to go to seminary (with a $15,000 annual tuition). Starting a *church* was a total risk.

But now those are the best things in my life. Good things come by way of risk. In fact, the bigger the risk, the bigger the reward. Look at your life and I bet you'll find the same.

Very little good happens in life without risk, so we need to start counting the reward. Rather than only playing out how bad things can go, we need to play out the good that can happen if we take the risk. Rather than being afraid of taking the risk, counting the cost will help us to be afraid of *not* taking the risk. We need to get to the place where our fear of missing out is greater than our fear of messing up.

We're so scared of regrets. And the truth is, if we take risks, we *will* have regrets. But they won't be as great as the regrets we would have for *not* taking those risks.

Like with the risks I've taken. My marriage was a risk. In marriage, are my wife and I always walking hand-in-hand through a field of flowers? No. Sometimes it's just not fun. We had our thirteenth anniversary recently, and we spent the entire day mad at each other. Hallmark doesn't make a card for that!

To my spouse, on our anniversary:

I wish you would die

a slow, painful death.

And please do it soon.

The best way I can picture spending tonight

is dancing on your grave.

And when we're not getting along, do I have regrets? Do I have thoughts like, "Man, my life would be easier if I weren't married"? Sure I do.

Or having kids—is that *always* a blast? Not so much. Sometimes it's just frustrating. And when that happens, do I have regrets? Do I have thoughts like, "What made me think I wanted to have kids?" Sure I do.

Or becoming a pastor and starting a church—is that always my dream job? No way. At times I dream of quitting. And when that happens, do I have regrets? Do I think, "Man, I could be making so much money now if I had stayed in law school," and "Why in the world did I start this church?" and "I would love to not have to deal with these people, 'cause they're all boneheads"? Sure I do!

See, when you take a risk, you will have regrets. *But the regrets that you experience for taking those risks are much smaller than the regrets you'd have for not taking those risks.* Isn't that right? Do I have regrets in marriage and being a parent? Yes. But would I have much greater regrets if I had never married my wife and had my kids? For sure!

And do I have regrets about becoming a pastor and starting a church? Yes. But would I have much greater regrets if I had never done it? Absolutely! See, when you take a risk, everything isn't going to be perfect, but it will still almost always be better than if you didn't take that risk.

That's why we need to fear missing out more than messing up. We need to count the reward. Willingness to risk is based on potential return.

A second way to get yourself to risk is to understand that faith *is* risk. Answer this question: what does faith *feel* like? Ever thought about that? What does faith feel like?

It feels like risk.

If you doubt that, read your Bible for a little bit. Seriously, can you name me some people in the Bible who had faith in God that *didn't* feel like risk? People of faith in the Bible were called to speak out against kings, lead huge groups of rebellious people, be spies, hide spies, face down a giant with a slingshot, move to unknown places, touch the contagious, and face death. Who in the Bible had faith and it didn't lead them to risk? I can't think of one. Risk is what faith is, what it does, and what it feels like. Faith is a risk, it leads to risk, and it feels like risk.

So if you're not taking any risks, are you really living by faith? If your life doesn't feel like risk, do you even have faith? If you don't take any risks, was your faith even necessary?

If you're not taking risks, isn't your faith kind of like that old car your friend has in the garage? You know the one; he bought it years ago and planned on fixing it up, but it's just been sitting there doing nothing for years. Does he have the car? Yes. But is he using it? Is it serving a purpose? Does anyone benefit from it? No, no, and no.

That's not the way we want to live. We want to live lives of faith. And faith *is* risk.

♥

A third factor we need to stay focused on is that without faith it is impossible to please God.[3] So if we don't live by faith, not only will we not be pleased, God won't be pleased either.

That ain't cool.

Without faith it is impossible to please God.

And I think it would be fair to say: without *risk* it is impossible to please God.

God is not looking for people who play it safe. Sometime read Hebrews 11. People call this chapter God's "Hall of Fame" or "Hall of Faith." God holds up his heroes from the Old Testament, the people he wants us to emulate. You'll notice that for each person, their *faith* is what God highlights. He gives an example of each person's faith. Why can God give examples? Because faith isn't just something that resides in your heart; it's something that causes you to *act*. God gives an example of each person's faith, and every example is of—yeah, you guessed it—*risk*.

Without risk it is impossible to please God.

As you consider taking some guerrilla action, as you inch out onto the ledge, as you realize how far down it is if you were to really jump, think of God looking at you with a smile on his face. Faith is risk, and risk pleases God. It makes him look at you and smile.

The fourth way to overcome fear and take the risk is to *make sure you're looking at God*.

One of the most famous risk stories in the Bible is David versus Goliath. Because we know how it turned out, what David did doesn't feel that risky to us, but for David it was a giant-sized risk to take on Goliath. It was a risk that none of the trained soldiers was willing even to consider, but David jumped at the chance.

When David shows up and learns that Goliath is mocking his God and his people, he immediately volunteers to fight him. What's interesting is that the first words we hear coming out of David's mouth are his asking what he'll receive for killing Goliath.[4] He wasn't counting the cost; he was counting the reward.

But what gave David the kind of confidence no one else had? If you read through the story you'll notice that David only refers to Goliath a few times, but he repeatedly talks about God. Over and over David exclaims that God is the one being defied, God is the one who gives victory, and God is the one who will be honored. From the time David laid eyes on Goliath, he couldn't stop talking about God. David sees the giant, mind you; he just sees God *more*.

What allows us to overcome fear and take risks is making sure we're looking at God. I have pictures of me at about age four in mid-flight jumping off a high dive at a swimming pool. The thing is that I climbed up the ladder, but I wouldn't jump off the board when I looked down. But then my father swam out to the spot where I'd be landing, so I focused on him . . . and jumped.

When you're looking at God, the giants that stand in your way just don't seem so big. The risks become manageable—not because we no longer fear but because we see something bigger than the risk. It's because we allow our faith to overcome our fear.

I read a great story about some guerrilla lovers. When he was college age, Pete Greig started a 24-7 prayer movement, trying to set up prayer rooms in different towns, where local Christians would pray around the clock. Pete started getting requests from people to speak in their town, or consult with their church, or start a new prayer room. One day he received a call asking him if he would come to Ibiza, Spain.

This request was more intriguing than most. Ibiza is one of five Spanish islands that together make up the Balearic enclave. Ibiza has been branded a modern-day Sodom and Gomorrah, known for depravity, drug-fueled excess, live sex shows, violence, rape, and sexual perversity.

Pete said yes.

He and three friends arrived in Ibiza a few months later and quickly adjusted their sleeping patterns so they could be awake all night and sleep all morning. They set up a prayer room in the middle of town and made sure someone was praying for the town 24-7. Every night they would go out in teams, making friends and gathering prayer requests on the streets and in the bars. They would often end the night helping drunk people find their way home or listening to people pour out their problems.

Soon their team grew. Those who could DJ got jobs in local bars. The entire group would regularly clean the beach of cans, used condoms, cigarette packets, and worse.

The Spectator, one of England's oldest satirical magazines, heard about the team and sent a reporter out to do a story.

The journalist, known for sarcastic treatments, wrote the following in her article entitled "Jesus Goes to the Disco":

I had hoped for solemn, pasty faces, biblical samplers and sensible shoes. Instead there were eyebrow rings, gelled hair and tanned skin. . . . At 4:00 a.m. when the bars begin to close and street cleaners start to hose the puke and urine off the pavement with neat bleach, an incongruously sober and cheery group appears. They stop and talk to the stragglers, ask lost girls if they are all right, unstuck passed-out teenagers from the street and heave them over to the taxi rank. Sometimes they ride home with them; occasionally they take a comatose boy to hospital. . . . Throughout the evening waitresses, seasonal workers, girls handing out flyers stopped group members in the street and poured out their problems. On the way to Café del Mar, a woman with bleached dreadlocks and bondage trousers, who looked as if she'd rather boil to death than be seen talking to a Christian, approached a girl named Claire. "I've finally been fired," she said, and offloaded fifteen minutes' worth of anxieties and frustrations. Outside a restaurant, a waitress stopped Becs Lindford and started worrying about her debt. "I want to go home, but I can't because the tax men will be on to me," she began, apropos of nothing, and continued for a further twenty minutes. Becs offered cheerful advice. Inside the restaurant, Jez, the director of a documentary about the group said, "People all over town are starting to talk about 24-7. I keep overhearing discussions about the work they're doing and their lives. They've had a huge impact."

Later, when interviewing someone for her story who had been watching the team, the journalist asked about them, "But isn't it terrifying for . . . everyone to go into town and confront drunken thugs?" The response: "Your readers won't like my answer—I don't imagine this sort of thing goes down very well in print—but they go out with confidence and purpose because they know in their hearts that they've been called here by God. He is with them; how can they be scared?"[5]

How do you overcome fear and take the risk? Make sure you're looking at God.

Are you feeling convinced? Whatever God's whispering for you to do, will you take the risk required to go guerrilla?

Let me tell you this: Taking the risk leads to guerrilla love. Taking the risk gives us the chance to become heroes. Taking the risk can change everything. It changes us, and it changes others.

Let's hit play on that Julio Diaz story again. Remember, he was in the subway station in the Bronx, just robbed at knifepoint by a teenage boy. As the boy walked away, Diaz called him back and offered him his coat. The boy asked, "Why are you doing this?" Diaz told the boy he must really need the money. Then he continued.

"I mean, all I wanted to do was get dinner, and if you really want to join me . . . hey, you're more than welcome."

This teenager looked at Diaz, paused, and agreed to go out to eat with him! Why? I have no idea. But my guess is that he was drawn by love.

So the two of them headed off to Diaz's favorite diner, and while they were eating, the manager, the dishwashers, and all the waiters came over to say hi to Diaz, who was everyone's favorite customer.

"You know everybody here," the teenager said. "Do you own this place?"

"No," Diaz responded, "I just eat here a lot."

"But you're even nice to the dishwasher."

"Well," Diaz replied, "haven't you been taught you should be nice to everybody?"

"Yeah, but I didn't think people actually behaved that way."

Diaz asked the teen what he wanted out of life but got only a sad look for an answer.

Finally the bill arrived and Diaz told the teen, "Look, I guess you're going to have to pay for this bill 'cause you have my money and I can't pay for this. So if you give me my wallet back, I'll gladly treat you."

The teen didn't even think about it, immediately returning Diaz's wallet.

Diaz paid for the meal and then gave the boy twenty dollars. But he asked for something in return: the knife, which the teen handed over.

Wow.

You or I would have given the robber our wallet, rushed home, and spent the rest of our lives complaining about how bad people are. Diaz took a risk, showed some guerrilla love, and helped to turn a bad person into someone at least a little bit better.

So as you crawl out on the ledge and you consider really doing whatever it is you've been considering, think about the reward; know that you're supposed to feel afraid, because faith *is* risk; listen for the heroes from Hebrews 11, who pleased God with their faith, as they call out to you, "Jump! Jump!"; and look down where you will see God smiling up at you, waiting to catch you.

How can you be scared?

Jump.

It's Time to Talk Guerrilla

1. In general, do you think of Christians as safe people or risky people?
2. If you think of Christians as typically the "play it safe" types, why do you think that is? Why might Christians, who have the mandate of God to risk and all

the resources of God at their disposal, choose to play it safe?

3. Read Matthew 25:14–30. If you had never heard this story and didn't know how it ended, and you only read verses 14–18, who would you assume Jesus would approve of: the two guys who basically gamble all of their master's money, or the guy who made sure he protected his master's money?

4. Do you really think of God as someone who approves of people taking huge risks, or does the idea of taking risks sound irresponsible to you and like something of which God would disapprove?

5. If someone said the principle we learn from the parable of the talents is, "Don't you dare avoid taking a risk with what God has given you!" would you agree with that? If not, why not?

6. When the servant who does not risk gives his explanation, he says, "I was afraid" (verse 25). In what ways has fear kept you from taking a risk you should have taken?

7. How can the principles in this chapter help you to overcome your fear and take the risk?

8. What is a risk or two God might be calling you to take?

It's Time to Get Guerrilla

Have you ever heard the question, "If money was no object and failure was not possible, what would you do for God?"

It's a good question. What risk would *you* love to take for God if you knew you couldn't fail and if money wasn't an issue?

The reason it's a good question is because if you take that risk, failure truly is not possible. We learn from Jesus (for instance in the parable of the talents, Matt. 25:14–30) that the only way to fail is by not taking the risk. Did you get that? The only way to fail is by not taking the risk God is calling you to take. So God may not make your endeavor a "success," but if you take the risk for him, you've *already* succeeded.

The other reason it's a good question is because money is *not* an issue. God has all the resources of the world at his disposal (see for instance Ps. 50:9–11) and can fully fund your endeavor if he chooses.

So let me ask again: what risk would you take for God now that you know money is not an issue and failure is not a possibility? And let me ask this: why aren't you taking that risk?

A bunch of excuses just came to mind, but can you recognize them for what they are—excuses? Can you see that they're driven by a fear of risk?

It's time to take the risk. You may think the risk is too big, but with God there is no such thing as big or small. God can do anything, and he's behind you. So jump. Take the risk. Do the thing you'd love to do for God.

Seriously.

For more assignments and ideas, and to learn about and become a part of the Guerrilla Lover movement, go to www .guerrillalovers.com.

21

LUNATIC FRINGE

Do you know anyone you think might be crazy? I'm not talking Mike Tyson, should-have-been-put-away-a-long-time-ago, certifiably-crazy crazy; I mean someone who mostly seems quite normal but still has something a little loony tunes about him or her. I'm not talking about your-uncle-who-lives-in-the-mountains-of-Tennessee-and-eats-squirrels-with-his-feet crazy; I mean someone who gets by just fine in life but still has this wild look in her eyes. I'm not talking yeah-you-can-see-him-but-visiting-hours-are-only-between-5:00-and-7:00-and-it-would-be-better-if-you-don't-have-any-sharp-objects-on-you-when-you-go-in crazy; I mean someone who can interact well with other people, yet everyone is just a bit nervous being around him.

Do you know anyone you think might be crazy?

I know a guy who wears a cape.

His name is Toni.

Yes, he would wear his cape to a costume party and to the premiere of a new Superman movie. But he also wears his cape mowing the lawn, and at the grocery store, and to his kids' soccer games.

He wears the cape all the time.

He also wears Heelys. Heelys are those sneakers that have wheels built into them so you basically roller-skate on them. What's cool is that you can't see the wheels, so they give the impression that the person is mysteriously floating along.

I asked Toni why he wears Heelys. He said it's because of the cape. The shoes help the cape to catch a little wind and create more of a superhero-swooping-in-to-save-the-day impression.

The first time I met with Toni, he showed up at the restaurant not wearing the cape. In the middle of breakfast he blurted out, "I wear a cape." Not having any experience responding to such admissions, I said, "Oh?"

Toni said, "Yeah, I didn't want to wear it because I was afraid it might freak you out."

Like having someone announce over pancakes that he wears a cape isn't going to freak me out.

When we left the restaurant Toni walked briskly to his car, immediately put on his cape, got in, and drove away.

I stared at him, wondering if maybe he was in such a hurry to get to his car because he was afraid his cape missed him. Or maybe he heard it calling him? And where was he headed to, Metropolis? Had he seen some kind of signal?

♥

What might hold you back from truly living life as a guerrilla lover? Perhaps it's that to obey God's call, to do what he's asking you to do, to do what love requires—it's gonna be a little crazy.

What you're considering doing, if you were to actually do it, well, *you* think it's crazy. And not only that, but other people will think it's crazy—will think *you're* crazy.

So let me tell you something that might surprise you: crazy is a good thing.

In fact, crazy is a *God thing*.

Don't believe me? Let me prove it to you.

In the Old Testament we read of times when God called people to speak for him, to deliver God's message to God's people. One time God called a guy named Isaiah. And God told Isaiah he needed to let the Egyptians and Cushites know that though things were going well for them now, they would be shamed because of their wrongdoing. Simple enough, right? Isaiah can just go to the place where everyone gathers to worship and give them the message. But that's not what God has in mind. Instead, God tells Isaiah to take off all his clothes and walk around naked as a sign to the people that they will be stripped of their power and be led into captivity with their buttocks exposed. And that's exactly what Isaiah did. He walked around naked (for three years!) as a sign to the Egyptians and Cushites.[1] I can picture some mother asking Isaiah if he would please cover his privates in front of her daughters and Isaiah looking rather sheepish and then saying apologetically, "I can't. God told me I have to do this."

Crazy.

Or how about this one: God called a guy named Ezekiel and told him to communicate to the people that they would suffer the consequences of their sin. So what's the plan? Ezekiel goes down to the center of town and preaches that message? Nope. God tells Ezekiel to go to the middle of town and lay on his left side for 390 days and then on his right side for 40 days. And he says that he wants Ezekiel to cook his food over burning human poop. Ezekiel is like, "Seriously, God? The laying on the side thing isn't bad enough, but *human* poop? Do I have to use human poop?" And God says, "Fine, Ezekiel, you can use cow poop." And that's exactly what Ezekiel does. He lays on his side for 430 days and, when hungry, cooks his food over burning cow patties.[2] I bet some local merchants came over and said that he was driving away business. Did he really have to lay there? It had been almost two years. And the smell of cooking poop? Could he please stop? Ezekiel would have shifted his weight, looked up, and said, "I can't. God told me I have to do this."

Crazy.

I'm just getting started. Some stories hint at God having some kind of split personality disorder. Like when God has Elijah's food delivered to him by ravens, which were a bird he had declared unclean. Or when Jesus's first miracle is turning 120 gallons of water into wine at a party, when all through the rest of the Bible he warns about the dangers of alcohol and prohibits drunkenness.

Crazy.

And look at the kind of people God chooses. Like the guy God points to and says, "There's a man after my own heart," and the dude is out in the street dancing in his underwear in front of a bunch of women. Or the guy God chooses to introduce his Son to the world, and he's this barbarian social outcast from the wilderness.

Crazy.

Now, I realize you may be uncomfortable with me calling God crazy. Sorry. Perhaps the real deal is that he's the only one who's sane. In the Bible God tells us, "For my thoughts are not your thoughts, neither are your ways my ways. . . . As the heavens are higher than the earth, so are my ways higher than your ways and my thoughts than your thoughts."[3] Maybe God's point is, "You all have lost it. I'm the only one still in possession of my marbles."

Maybe, but I'm going to keep us on edge and stick with the uncomfortable idea that God is crazy. And from what I've seen, he's looking for crazy people, and he calls them to do crazy things.

Another way of saying the same idea is that God is uncivilized. God is uncivilized, he calls uncivilized people, and he asks them to do uncivilized things. Maybe you've heard the expression, "The revolution will not be televised." Well, we've been talking about the revolution of God, and it will *not* be civilized.

But that's exactly what we've tried to do to it, and it's exactly the problem. Somehow we've gotten civilized. We've come to believe that Christians are people who behave and dress right and have good manners and act dignified and are respectable, which is basically a load of crap. Jesus didn't get crucified for being respectable. He was crucified because people thought he was crazy, and a crazy man leading an uncivilized revolution is a very dangerous thing. And God has not called us to be dignified; he's called us to be crazy and to use guerrilla tactics to turn the world upside down. God is not calling us to be respectable. He's calling us to the lunatic fringe.

If you're afraid of doing crazy things, afraid of others thinking you're insane, you will never truly become a guerrilla lover. God is a crazy God who calls crazy people to do crazy things.

And it's time for us to get crazy.

♥

Remember my friend Toni in the cape? When we last saw Toni he was speeding away from a restaurant. That day at the restaurant I asked him not only why he wore Heelys but also why he wore a cape. I'll never forget his answer: "When people see someone in a cape, they expect something great to happen. And that's the person I want to be."

I wanted to tell him that when people see someone in a cape, they actually expect something *crazy* to happen, but I didn't dare. And I don't know; maybe most of the great things that happen are kind of crazy.

I love Toni's attitude. He's saying, "I'm not supposed to be a normal person. I'm connected to a supernatural God. I have supernatural power available to me, supernatural compassion that drives me, a supernatural cause to advance. I'm supposed to be a hero. That's my calling because I follow the ultimate hero. So if wearing a cape lets people know there's a hero around, I'll wear a cape. If wearing a cape reminds me that when I show up, it's to serve others, I'll wear a cape. If wearing a cape is a mark of greatness, then I'll wear a cape, because I've been marked by the Great One."

Talking to Toni, I started to get into this idea. (But no, to answer your question, I have not started wearing a cape. I do, however, wear spandex pants. Baby steps . . .) So I began asking him all kinds of questions. How do people respond to the cape? What do you say? Do you machine wash the cape? How many capes do you own? And finally, could you tell me about some of the great things you've done in your cape?

Toni was very hesitant to share stories, afraid he might appear proud. He said things like, "It's no big deal. I just think we need to act in love all the time and force people to ask why." But I kept prying and finally got to hear some stories of his guerrilla lovin'. I heard about how he regularly takes homeless people to lunch, how he stops to help broken-down motorists, and how he volunteers with kids every week in his church's children's ministry.

One story really struck me. Toni explained that one day he was pulling out of a parking lot when he saw a homeless person sitting on the corner. He was a raggedy looking guy, about thirty years old, holding a big cardboard sign on which he had written, "Look at me, I'm stupid." Toni kept driving, but then the words on the sign registered. He says he had a prompting, a repeating thought: *He's not stupid. He's valued by God. He's not stupid. He's valued by God.* Then another thought: *Go back and tell him.* So Toni circled back around the block and parked his van. He dug through his work materials in the back, finding some cardboard and a marker. Toni admits that he paused before he left his van, wondering how he might be perceived by passing motorists and what the other homeless people might do. But then he got out, went over to the man, and introduced himself. And Toni proposed an unusual deal. He offered to give the man all the money in his wallet to let him change his sign. The man agreed. Toni got out his wallet, paid him all his money, and changed the man's sign. Then Toni went back to his car, and as he drove away he looked and saw the man standing with a big smile on his face, holding his sign which now read, "Look at me, I'm beautiful."

I've got to tell you, when I heard that story, I was so moved I had to fight back tears. I also had to hold back my laughter. What must that homeless guy have thought when he saw Toni come gliding up to him, rolling along in his Heelys, cape flapping in the wind? Picturing it makes me laugh so hard my stomach hurts.

But seriously, if guerrilla love had a graphic, it might be that homeless man holding up his new sign, with Toni fluttering away in his cape. In fact, I propose we give Toni the first ever Guerrilla Lover Award for that one.

You know, the more I think about it, the more I think that none of this is crazy. In fact, I've decided what I think is crazy: crazy is continuing to live the way you have. Albert Einstein said insanity is doing the same things expecting a different result. Insanity isn't trying something great for God; it's doing the same old things, living the same old way, and expecting that somehow your life is going to become great and you're going to begin having a great impact for God.

So do something different!

Do something crazy for God!

Join the lunatic fringe!

It may be the sanest thing you can possibly do.

In fact, if your deal in life has been *I'm a Christian, so I'm respectable*, I'd love to pay you to hold up a new sign: *I'm a Christian, so I'm crazy*.

It's Time to Talk Guerrilla

1. Apple Computers had a commercial back in 1997 that said, "Here's to the crazy ones, the misfits, the rebels,

the troublemakers, the round pegs in a square hole, the ones who see things differently. They're not fond of rules, and they have no respect for the status quo. You can quote them, disagree with them, glorify or vilify them. About the only thing you can't do is ignore them, because they change things. They push the human race forward, and while some may see them as the crazy ones, we see genius, because the people who are crazy enough to think they can change the world are the ones who'll do it."

(a) Let's pretend that was a commercial for Jesus. Do you think it's an accurate description of Jesus? Why or why not?

(b) Now let's pretend it's a commercial for *you*. Does it accurately describe you? In what ways?

2. Read 1 Corinthians 4:9–13. What do you think it means to be a "fool for Christ"?

3. Apparently Christians were once considered fools, dishonored, the scum of the earth. Today Christians are generally considered dignified, conservative, respectable, boring goody-goodies. In what ways does this passage make you think, "Wow, I've really got to change my thinking on what it means to be a follower of Jesus"?

4. Oswald Chambers wrote, "The only explanation for a Christian's life has to be the existence of God. Otherwise it makes no sense."[4]

(a) What about your life doesn't make sense apart from your faith in God?

(b) If you can't think of an answer for that last question, maybe this will be a better place to start: What about your life do you wish made no sense apart from your faith in God?

5. Take some time to pray, asking God to make you crazy. Let him know that if you're supposed to be not just a follower of Christ but a fool for him too, you're willing and ready to go.

It's Time to Get Guerrilla

Are you afraid that you're about to be challenged to get crazy?

You are.

Let's think about signs. In this chapter we heard about Toni, who changed a man's sign. And something seems to make crazy people like to hold up signs—you know, "The End Is Near" kind of stuff.

So what kind of guerrilla lover sign could you make and hold up? Would it seem crazy to hold a sign out in public? Probably so. Is that a bad thing? Not necessarily. And your assignment is just that. You're going to make a sign, and you're going to hold it up out in public for people to see. Think of it as an experiment in being a fool for Christ.

Now, it wouldn't take much creativity to make a sign that says, "Accept Jesus" or "John 3:16," and it also probably wouldn't have much of an impact. So let's be more creative than that, and let's try to think of a sign that will actually be intriguing and provoke some thought. So what will your sign say? And where will you hold it up?

By the way, I know that right now you're thinking, *There is absolutely no way that I'm going to make a sign and hold it up on some street corner.* And that's exactly why you *are* going to do this! C'mon, get crazy! Do it. Shake up your life a little. This is something you've never done and will probably never do again. So do it.

By the way, when you do it, have someone take a picture of you. Then go to www.guerrillaloversbook.com and post it on the "People Holding Signs" page. Let the rest of us see you being crazy!

Now go do it.

For more assignments and ideas, and to learn about and become a part of the Guerrilla Lover movement, go to www.guerrillalovers.com.

INSURGENT INTEGRATION

Let's say that you know God's calling you to practice guerrilla lovefare, you want to obey, and you're even willing to take a crazy risk. So what's going to stop you?

You live a microwave life.

And you have a TV-dinner faith.

♥

I am old enough (just barely!) to remember when we got our first microwave. The Little League team I was playing for was sponsored by an appliance store, and I think the owner gave my father a discount. He brought the microwave home, and we all stared in amazement at this little box. We basked in the glow of the light that came on when we opened it. We were told to keep our distance when it was running. It didn't have a spinning tray—that would come later—but the thing cooked things faster than Angelina Jolie can adopt a third-world baby. TV dinners, which used to take thirty minutes in the oven, now took less than five. It was incredible.

What's ironic is that now a microwave can't cook fast enough for us. I stare at it in anger. How long does it take to cook a freakin' Hot Pocket?

And it's that way with everything, isn't it? When I was a kid, if I wanted to learn when the microwave was invented, I had to go to the library and read it in an encyclopedia. Today I do a search on my laptop computer, but I get totally frustrated if the Internet is running slow, forcing me to wait ten seconds for the answer. How long does it take to get an answer on this freakin' computer?

When I was younger I hated phone numbers with 9s and 0s in them because it was unbelievable how long it took for the rotary dial on the phone to come back around on those numbers. Today I get annoyed when my cell phone takes a few extra seconds to connect. How long does it take for this freakin' phone to beam my call up into outer space, connect with a satellite, beam it back down to someone else's phone, and have that person answer?

Everything is getting faster and faster, but nothing will ever move fast enough for us. The number of things we need to do continually increases, the margin we have in our lives continually decreases, and this will be what you use as an excuse not to become a guerrilla lover: you don't have the time.

I can hear you saying it right now. "This all sounds great, and I'm in favor of it. I even believe it would improve my life and allow me to have a much greater impact on the world, but I'm so busy. My schedule is already overfilled. I'm overcommitted as it is. I really don't have the time. I . . . just . . . don't . . . have . . . the . . . time!"

So let's talk about your priorities.

One time someone asked Jesus what he should do to inherit eternal life. Jesus asks what he thinks the law teaches. The man replies with the Jesus creed: love God and love my neighbor. Jesus commends him, but the man isn't through. He pushes Jesus further by asking, "And who is my neighbor?"[1] In response Jesus gives him a story.

Jesus tells of a man who gets jacked up like Rodney King at a policeman's ball ("Can't we all just get along?") and is left for dead. And some guys come along who look like him and who he'd consider friends, but they leave him for dead. Then this other dude who looks different and talks different, who this guy would look at like a KKK member looks at an NAACP advocate, walks up and totally takes care of him. This is not an "Are you okay? Do you want me to call someone on my cell phone for you?" obligatory stop. No, this dude picks him up, takes him to a good, safe place to stay, and cares for his wounds. And as if that wasn't enough, the dude has to leave, but he leaves a bunch of money to make sure the guy continues to be taken care of.

So who does Jesus identify as the "neighbor" we have to love? Well, apparently everyone, even someone we might view as an enemy.

And what does it look like to love them? Well, it looks guerrilla.

So let's review.

1. Religious guy asks Jesus what is most important.
2. Jesus tells him it's loving people, even our enemies, with an audacious, serving, caring, uncomfortable kind of love. The only higher priority is loving God.

So tell me again how you don't have time to do this. Seriously?

Jesus says that being a guerrilla lover is so vital that only one thing—loving God—is more important, but you don't have time for it?

Here's where it gets really disturbing. After Jesus tells the question-asking guy to love God and love people, he tells him, "Do this and you will live."[2] Now, I may be reading too much into this story, but I'm pretty sure the guy who asked the question *was alive.* Jesus seems to be insinuating here that it's possible to live without really living.

I have to be uncomfortably honest and tell you that I've had stretches of my life where I lived without really living. And I look back and wonder, *Why was I willing to settle for life-less life?* Some of those times came *before* I started following Jesus, so that's excusable. But some of them came *after*, when I knew the path to really living was to love God and love people, and I just didn't do it. Either I drifted apart from God, or I was okay with God but didn't really love people. Oh, I would have *said* I loved people, but did my love for people look anything like this picture Jesus gives us of what loving people really looks like? Not at all. Why?

Well, sometimes it was because I was just too busy.

Too busy to love people. Too busy to get guerrilla.

Think about it: what that means is that I was too busy "living" to actually live.

I bet you've been there too, and maybe you're living it right now. You've had thoughts of "I need to mend that relationship with her" or "I need to start serving at my church" or "I should volunteer at that hospital" or "I should sign up to coach my son's team this season," but then you think, "I can't do that. I'm too busy. I just . . . don't have . . . the time!"

You're too busy living to actually live.

Is that you? If you haven't felt very alive for a while now, is it because you don't "have" the time to do the things that bring life?

If so, when will you start making the time to really live? After you die?

Things aren't going to change. Your schedule isn't going to clear up; people aren't going to stop asking you to do things; your workload won't decrease.

What's going to stop you from living guerrilla? Perhaps that you live a microwave life.

But it also may be that you have a TV dinner faith.

I grew up eating a lot of TV dinners. Probably partly because they were cheap . . . and also because they were quick. Only thirty minutes! Until the microwave showed up, and then five minutes wasn't fast enough. Now I realize that most people don't call them TV dinners anymore—now they're "frozen meals" or "microwave meals"—and I think the reason it changed is because now we'll eat any meal in front of the TV. And other things have changed about the TV dinner. The tray used to be made out of aluminum, whereas it's now a microwavable plastic. And you can find healthy versions now, as opposed to in the past. But one thing about TV dinners hasn't changed, and I doubt it ever will.

I suspect that the TV dinner will be the last place in America where segregation is acceptable.

Isn't it true? We've had the civil rights movement, we've desegregated our schools, even South Africa has seen the end of apartheid, but still there is a wall between my peas and my Salisbury steak! When, O God, will this segregation cease?

Now every once in a while you'll see a pea has escaped the pea area; somehow it jumped the wall or took the Underground Railroad into mashed potatoes territory. As you open your dinner the pea is standing there, frozen with fear, trying not to be seen, like, "Oh no, I've been caught!"

It's cool that a radical pea or two has gotten the courage to make a run for freedom, but I can't wait for the day when some pea or carrot with vision and leadership ability will seek equality for all the TV dinner foods. I can just picture him standing on top of the other vegetables so all the food from the other sections can see and hear as he shouts out:

> I have a dream. I have a dream that one day this TV dinner will rise up and live out the true meaning of its creed: "We hold these truths to be self-evident: that all foods are created equal." I have a dream that one day on the big section of the Swanson tray the sons of chicken breasts and the sons of green beans will be able to be eaten together at the table of brotherhood.

I have a dream that one day even the spaghetti dinner, a dinner sweltering with the sauce of injustice, sweltering with the zucchini vegetable medley of oppression, will be transformed into a goulash of freedom and justice.

I have a dream that these four little peas will one day live in a tray where they will not be judged by their food group but by their nutritional content. I have a dream today.

And if the TV dinner is to be great, this must become true. So let freedom ring from the prodigious slices of lasagna. Let freedom ring from the mighty meatloaf of the Hungry-Man meal. Let freedom ring from the heightening mashed potatoes of Stouffer's. Let freedom ring from the apple crisp of Banquet.

And when this happens, when we allow freedom to ring, when we let it ring from every main entrée, from every vegetable and every dessert compartment, we will be able to speed up the day when all of God's foods, fried chicken and cranberry compote, Swedish meatballs and Mandarin shrimp, cheesy broccoli and French bread pizza, will be able to join hands and sing in the words of the old Negro spiritual, "Free at least! Free at last! Thank God Almighty, we are free at last!"

The TV dinner may be the last place in America where segregation is acceptable, except that we also accept it in our lives. We tend to approach God and spiritual life like a TV dinner. We put walls between things and compartmentalize our lives. Don't you?

I mean, we feel convicted about needing to make a difference in the world, and our response is to sign up for a mission trip. We know we're supposed to do something locally, so we sign up for the free car wash our church is putting on. And nothing is wrong with going on a mission trip or participating in a community service event; in fact, doing that is fantastic. What's a problem is if we go on that mission trip or do the community service event and then return home feeling like we were obedient to God, but our lives weren't really changed, and we go back to life as usual.

Do you see it?

What we did was good, but it's like we jumped into a different compartment where we served and were all missional, but then we jumped back into the normal life compartment. And that's *not* what God is after. He wants to create a life that is, not a life that does. He wants us to not just do a mission trip but be missionaries. He wants us to not just do a service project but become servants. His goal is to knock down our walls and blend everything together into a transformed life. He wants us to have a different lifestyle.

And one of the most significant signs that we have a TV dinner life is our favorite excuse for not serving, "I don't have enough time. I'm just too busy." What does that reveal? Not only that we're living at microwave speed with messed-up priorities, but also that we haven't incorporated guerrilla love into our everyday lives but instead feel like it's something we must add. It's another compartment, and I'm having enough trouble jumping between the ones I already have!

So what if, as insurgents committed to our revolution, we started living integrated lives? What if we started blending things together? What if . . .

What if every time you mow your yard, you also mowed the yard of one of your neighbors? Or what if you brought their garbage can to the garage when you get yours? Or what if every time you buy hygiene products for yourself, you purchased an extra set to donate to a homeless shelter? Or what if every night while you watch TV, you wrote two encouragement notes? Or what if instead of paying at the pump, you paid inside and started developing a friendship with the guy who works there? Or what if every time you make a cake, or pie, or lasagna, you made a second and brought it to a neighbor? Or what if instead of going grocery shopping by yourself, you picked up an elderly woman who lives on her own and brought her along? Or what if instead of bringing in your cup of coffee to the office every morning, you also brought in an extra cup for someone else?

What else could you do? Well, I'm not sure because I don't know what you *already* do. Think through your days. What do you do alone where you could include someone else? What do you do for yourself that you could do for someone else at the same time? How do you spend money on yourself that you could also spend on someone else?

See how a guerrilla lover should be something you *are*, not something you add to your life? It's not another thing to do in your day; it permeates your day because it's your identity, and a priority, and what will allow you to experience real life before you die.

It's time to break down the walls, mix your life all up, and sing from the top of your lungs, "Free at least! Free at last! Thank God Almighty, I am free at last!"

It's Time to Talk Guerrilla

1. Before reading this chapter, was the "I don't have time" excuse already one you were making when reading this book?
2. This chapter brings back the "Jesus creed" from an earlier chapter: "Love God, love people."
   (a) How good a job have you been doing at making the Jesus creed your creed?
   (b) If you were put on trial for being a "love God, love people" person, what would be the best evidence for it? What would be the best evidence against it?
3. Do you agree that real life comes through loving God and loving people? Why or why not?
4. Is it possible that you've been too busy living to really live? How does your busyness keep you from loving God and loving people?
5. How does the TV dinner metaphor apply to your life? How do you see yourself segregating the "love God"

and "love people" aspects of your life from the rest of your life?

6. In what "segments" of your life do you find it easiest to love God and love people?

7. In what "segments" of your life do you find it most difficult to love God and love people?

8. Read 1 Corinthians 10:31; Colossians 3:17; and Colossians 3:23.

9. Do you see how God's plan is for you to desegregate your life and make the whole thing about loving God and loving people? What might that look like today and tomorrow and the day after that?

It's Time to Get Guerrilla

This project is going to take you a while to complete, but it could be life changing. Here are the steps:

1. Monitor your time for the next fourteen days. Write down how you spend every half hour. This may get tiresome, but stick with it.

2. At the end of the two weeks, take a close, hard look at how you spend your time. What surprises you the most? What are you spending too much time on? What are you not spending enough time on?

3. Have you tried the exercise where you have a pile of several large rocks and a bunch of small stones and have to fit them all in a bucket? If you put the small stones in first, the big rocks will not fit in the bucket. However, if you put the big rocks in first, the small stones will fill in all the empty spaces, and everything will fit in. If you are going to live out the Jesus creed (love God and love people) and live as a guerrilla lover, what are the "big rocks" that you must first put in your schedule to make sure they aren't pushed out?

4. Write down an ideal schedule for the next two weeks. Put in the big rocks first (times to focus on loving God and times to focus on loving people), and then see how much time you have left to work, sleep, exercise, watch TV, and so on.

5. Look back through how you lived your last two weeks again. This time think through how you could have loved God and loved people in *everything* you did. How could you have loved God and loved people . . .

   (a) at work?
   (b) when you took out the garbage?
   (c) while you exercised?
   (d) during your time at the grocery store?
   (e) when you were driving home from work?
   (f) as you watched TV?

For more assignments and ideas, and to learn about and become a part of the Guerrilla Lover movement, go to www .guerrillalovers.com.

SIMPLE OBEDIENCE

My friend Jud is the pastor of an amazing church in Henderson, Nevada, a suburb of Las Vegas. He tells about a guy named Cody. Cody was a tournament bass pro fisherman who was so good he had been featured on ESPN. He was well on his way to becoming a millionaire but then got caught up in a crack addiction. He soon went through his entire savings buying crack, and then he sold his Harley, then his car, then his house, and finally his boat. He lost everything to his drug addiction. Eventually he ended up homeless, living in the field next to Jud's church.

Cody would get up each morning, wash windows until he had enough money to score some crack, buy it, and then spend the rest of the day in that field, high. He lived that way for eight straight months. Cody is naturally a pretty big guy, but his weight dropped to 130 pounds. After he went three months in a row without bathing, the homeless started avoiding him. Cody later said, "You know it's bad when homeless people think you smell."

One of the other homeless said, "Listen, this church here will feed you on Sunday mornings and let you take a shower. You should check it out."

Cody was anti-God, anti-Christianity, anti-faith. The idea of walking into a church repulsed him, but not as much as his body odor did. So that Sunday morning he tentatively walked into the church building. He didn't want to think about where he was and didn't want anyone in the church to acknowledge him. But a member of the church named Michelle happened to be facing that direction and couldn't help but notice the shell of a man who had just walked through the door. He was filthy and emaciated, with a long scraggly beard falling from his face. As she looked him over she sensed God saying to her, "You need to go talk to him." She resisted for a second but knew God was telling her to do it and she had to obey. So she timidly walked over to Cody and said, "You look like you need a hug."

Cody later said, "She didn't know it, but at that moment all I really wanted to do was put a gun to my head and blow my brains out. I mean, I had eaten at fine restaurants. I had socialized with celebrities. And now I was eating out of garbage cans."

Cody looked over this woman, who appeared to be a very ordinary soccer mom. He couldn't help but notice her smile. But still he said, "Lady, I don't smell very good. You don't want to be near me."

Michelle looked in his eyes, got closer, and said, "Jesus loves you," and she gave Cody a hug.

Cody said in that moment, for the first time in his life, God began to soften his heart and break through. He was so stunned that this lady would come up to him, even with how horrible he appeared and how disgusting he smelled, and hug him, that his heart opened to the possibility that maybe there really was a God.

That hug launched Cody on a journey. He decided to stay for the church service. Then he went to the church library and checked out a Bible. He kept coming back. And soon Cody gave his life to Christ. He was still living in the field, but he says he was the happiest homeless guy in Las Vegas. In fact, other homeless people would say, "You must have got some good drugs. What are you on?" and he would smile and say, "I'm on Jesus, man."

What I love most about that story is that it was all because Michelle was willing to obey what she felt God was calling her to do.

We've talked a lot about guerrilla love. In fact, we're almost done with this journey we've been taking together. And we've been thinking about the reasons we might not do what we're supposed to do—it's too risky, we'll seem crazy, we don't have the time. But probably the main reason we won't is simply this: *we don't want to.*

See, I know something about you that you don't want me to know: you are selfish. And so am I. It's the fundamental defect in the basic operating system of human beings. We are self-centered, self-absorbed, self-idolizing, self-indulgent, self-obsessed.

Don't believe me? Think about this: when you're in a group picture and someone shows you that photo and asks what you think, what do you look for first?

Yourself.

If you look good, "It's a great picture!" Every single other person can be cross-eyed, tongues hanging out, pants just dropped to their feet, but if you look good, "It's a great picture!" Don't deny it, you know it's true.

This selfishness can taint everything we do. I walk around life like it's a movie about me. The rest of you are extras who can easily be replaced. The plot line is all about me because I am so undeniably great.

And this is why guerrilla lovefare is a problem. It doesn't focus on me. It forces me to focus on others. It doesn't serve me;

it serves others. And I seemingly get nothing out of it. In fact, I have to *give*. What I'm supposed to do often makes me feel uncomfortable. And I *really* don't like being uncomfortable.

So probably the main reason we won't engage in guerrilla love is . . . we don't want to.

The problem with all this is that in reality, outside my delusional make-believe world where I am the featured star, I am *not* the greatest. God is. And life only fits with reality, it only makes sense and works, when I focus on God and serve God, even if I seem to be getting nothing out of it and it makes me uncomfortable.

The main reason we won't do guerrilla love is because we don't want to, but the main reason we *must* is because God wants us to. And we simply need to obey.

The Bible says a lot about obeying God. God commands it,[1] it's the source of receiving his blessing,[2] and it's what proves we truly love Jesus.[3] We don't like the idea of obedience (unless someone has to obey *me*—now that I can go for!), and we tend to make Christianity and following Jesus very complicated. I wonder if we make it so complicated because we don't like the idea of obedience.

We should be guerrilla lovers because God commands it. All the excuses we use really don't add up to anything, because we need to simply obey God.

I love the simplicity of this statement from Scripture: "The only thing that counts is faith expressing itself through love."[4] That's powerful. The *only* thing that counts? Only?

God has commanded us to express our faith through love.

But will we obey?

I wish my life was an uninterrupted pattern of simple obedience to God, but it isn't. Because I am so selfish, there have been times when I didn't obey. When God was calling me to do some guerrilla lovin' and I said no.

I think about phone calls I had a prompting to make, but didn't. People I felt like I should offer assistance to, but didn't. Neighbors I was supposed to invite to church, but didn't.

And I know it. The thing I *don't* know is what the impact of my disobedience has been. To be honest, that's something I don't want to know.

Because I know that every time I *have* obeyed, God has used it in great ways.

I think back to when I was in law school and felt like God was pushing me to go into ministry instead. Selfish Vince reared his ugly head and thought, *I have a full scholarship. I am paying nothing to attend law school and will graduate with no school loans. The average salary coming out of this law school is $80,000. I'm better than average! On the other hand, it will cost me about $15,000 a year to go to seminary. The average salary coming out is about $20,000. This is insanity!*

But God was asking me, so I cut off the ugly head of Selfish Vince and transferred to seminary. And nothing against attorneys—the world needs more of them (like I need more holes in my head!) (insert your favorite lawyer joke here)—but when I think back on that decision, it was so right. The impact I've made for God as a pastor versus what I would have made . . . wow. And that impact happened because I simply obeyed.

After seminary I did a one-year internship at a huge church. As the internship concluded they let me know I could stay on as a permanent staff member. It was a great church and the salary exceeded my expectations. They even offered a full set of benefits. I also received an offer from a new church outside of Washington, DC. The church had about 80 people. The salary they offered was $12,000 less. But, they explained, they actually couldn't afford to pay me anything; I would have to try to raise my own salary. The benefits that came with this job were, well, I would get to learn firsthand how to raise my own salary! Selfish Vince told me it was an obvious decision, but I prayed, and God told me to say yes to the new church. So once again I decapitated Selfish Vince and moved to Washington, DC. The impact we had at that church, where we grew by hundreds in two years, and the experience I received were incredible. And that impact happened because I simply obeyed.

Things were going amazingly well at that new church; in fact, after two years they told me that they could finally pay me. So I left. Selfish Vince was all excited about having a guaranteed paycheck and finally being able to feel comfortable. But God whispered to me that I wasn't supposed to feel comfortable, that he had given me the experience in that new church for a reason. And so we moved to Virginia Beach to start a brand-new church. I've been here now for eleven years, and the impact has been incredible. And that impact has happened because I simply obeyed.

I look back and see that every time I've ignored Selfish Vince and obeyed God, it's led to crazy amounts of impact. That makes me want to always obey, because I dream about being a part of changing the world.

But actually obeying isn't always so easy. In fact, recently I've had one of my most difficult challenges in obeying God.

It all started on Thanksgiving Day 2007 when I decided to take our new puppy for a walk. We were going though my neighborhood when all of a sudden I was overwhelmed with this thought, like I heard a voice inside of me that said, "You need to start a church in Las Vegas."

The first thing that was bizarre about this is that I'm not one for hearing voices. Yes, I totally believe God still speaks to us today, but still, I don't hear a lot of voices. In fact, I tend to be cynical about people who say they hear voices. I call them things like *crackpots*, *cuckoo for Cocoa Puffs*, and, um, you know, *voice-hearers*.

The second thing that was bizarre was the message from said voice. If the voice had said, "Go home and order a pizza.

I mean, sure, it's only ten in the morning, but Thanksgiving dinner is still hours away," I'd have thought, "Wow, I have the best voice ever! I wish my voice gave me advice more often." Or if my voice had said, "Today in the economy, the Dow dropped by another eighty points," I would have said, "Wait a second—last night when I was sleeping, did someone implant a radio transistor into my brain? Because I believe I'm picking up some kind of news report."

But the voice said, "You need to start a church in Las Vegas."

Sure, the fact that I've started a church shows I'm *capable* of it, but the fact that I've started a church is also why I knew I'd never do it again. It was hard enough the first time.

And if I was going to start a church, it *wouldn't* be in Las Vegas. I'm an East Coast guy, through and through. All my friends and family are on the East Coast. And I don't care if it is a dry heat—105 degrees is 105 degrees.

So I decided to ignore the voice. The only problem was that I knew the voice was from God. I knew it.

The rest of the day (and the next day, and the rest of the week) I couldn't stop thinking about starting a church in Las Vegas. Finally I shared what the voice had told me with my wife, Jen. I expected her to get emotional, but instead she very nonchalantly said, "Whatever."

"Whatever?" I was emotional. "What do you mean, 'whatever'?"

"We are *not* starting a church in Las Vegas," she answered.

"That's right!" I was agreeing with her like Charlton Heston at an NRA rally. "We are *not* going!"

"Do you really think it was God?" she asked.

"Well, um, yeah. It was God."

"So," she asked, "what are you going to do about it?"

"Nothing," I answered. "I'm *not* starting another church, *especially* in Las Vegas."

"But God told you."

"Yeah, but . . ." I paused. "He'd have to tell me several more times to get me to even think about it."

Jen started walking out of the room.

"How do we know it wasn't our weirdo neighbor?" I shouted after her. "He might be a ventriloquist! Or maybe it was the dog! Can you prove that this dog *can't* talk? I mean, we've only had him for a couple weeks. We don't know . . ."

Unfortunately, I kept thinking about it. Every day I would mention it to my wife. I'd say things like, "Why do you think God said that to me?" "Do you think maybe it's because I'm good at connecting with people who are far from God, and there are probably a lot of them in Las Vegas?" "But if we moved to Las Vegas, we'd never see our family." "Maybe God told me that because my father ruined his life, my childhood, and my parents' marriage in Las Vegas."

I kept mentioning it, and every time I did, Jen would roll her eyes and say, "Whatever." But one day I said something about it again and she burst into tears, ran upstairs, and hid underneath the blankets of our bed. So I ran upstairs after her. "Why are you crying?"

Jen sobbed, "Because we're moving to Las Vegas!"

"No, we're not!" I was disagreeing with her like Charlton Heston at a PETA rally.

"Yes, we are," Jen blubbered out. "God told me we're supposed to go."

"No, I told God he has to tell me in several other ways."

Jen pulled down the blanket, looked at me, and said, "Whatever." Only this time "whatever" had a whole new meaning.

Two months later I went on a trip to Israel with a group of pastors. One day we were riding in a bus through Israel when the guy in front of me turned around and said, "Hey Vince, I know someone who is looking for a church planter for Las Vegas. Would you be open to starting a new church in Las Vegas? You'd be perfect for it."

Unbelievable.

But I still wouldn't obey.

Then the next month another pastor and I were interviewed for a church planting conference. A Christian film crew flew up from Florida to interview us. They filmed us talking for about an hour. Then the director dude said, "I have all I need, but I just have to get a few shots of you guys talking from different angles. I'm not going to be recording the audio, so you can talk about whatever you want while I film. Go ahead."

I asked, "Well, what should we talk about?"

"Talk about whatever you want," he answered.

"That's weird, though," I said. "Give us a topic."

"Fine," he said, "I'll give you a topic." He put the camera right up to my face and said, "Vince, what do you think about moving to Las Vegas and starting a new church on the Las Vegas strip? And if you were to do that, what would it look like?"

I said, "Dude, turn off your camera."

"No," he replied. "Don't talk to me; talk to each other about that."

"No," I said. "You turn off your camera. Why did you say that? Is this some sort of joke? Who told you?"

He looked confused. "No, it's just that there's no church on the Las Vegas strip, and I think it's the place that needs church the most. So I think someone needs to start one there, and you seem like the kind of guy who could do it."

Unbelievable.

Throughout this time period I began confiding in a few trusted friends and asking for their advice. I expected them to tell me to stay where I was, but every one said, "You need to go out and start a church in Las Vegas."

A few encouraged me to fly out to Vegas and pray there, so finally I got on a plane and spent three days there by myself.

I prayed through the list of reasons *not* to go: (1) I love the church I'm at. (2) I've planned on staying in Virginia Beach my entire life. (3) All my friends are here. (4) I get to work with the best staff in the world. (5) I love living in Virginia Beach. (6) It's the only home my kids have ever known. (7) Growing up, I hated moving, and I don't want to do that to my kids. (8) And I certainly don't want to raise my kids in Las Vegas. (9) My wife and I are East Coast people. (10) Our families are here; we drive to see them. If we live in Vegas, that's not going to happen. (11) It's 140 freakin' degrees in Las Vegas! (12) The cost of living is higher in Las Vegas. (13) I'd have to start a church all over again; it's the hardest thing I've ever done. (14) I'd have to go back to square one (no staff, no resources, etc.). (15) I've been told by several pastors who have great churches in the suburbs of Las Vegas that the strip would be the most difficult place in the country to start a new church. One called it a "suicide mission."

And the list went on and on.

Then I prayed through the list of reasons *to* go: (1) God told me.

Yeah, that was about it.

But it was like I heard a voice again, a silent but strong and encouraging voice, and it said, "That's reason enough."

And so finally I said yes. Finally I obeyed. And even though I'm incredibly sad to leave my church and friends and family, still I can't wait to see how God will use this new church. And whatever impact he'll allow me to have, it will all be because I simply (and finally) obeyed.

Speaking of Las Vegas, let's go back to Cody's story.

Remember, he was the successful tournament bass fisherman who developed a crack addiction. He lost everything and became homeless, but one Sunday he walked into a church, and soon his life was changed.

Fast-forward four years: Cody is married, owns a successful business, and is doing great. If you met him you'd never know he spent eight months sleeping in a field. During those four years the mayor of Las Vegas made a law that people could no longer feed the homeless in a public place. Cody couldn't believe it. He felt God leading him to do something. So Cody hired an attorney and took on the mayor and his legal staff. They went to court, with Cody challenging the law on grounds that it was unconstitutional.

Just picture the scene: On one side of the courtroom you have the mayor and all his lawyers in their high-powered suits. On the other side sits Cody, in his street clothes, and the one attorney he could afford to hire.

The judge listened to the arguments, looked over the materials, and declared the law unconstitutional. Today you can feed a homeless person in Las Vegas—you can show them guerrilla love—and it's because of Cody.

And remember, it all goes back to a woman named Michelle, standing in her church lobby, who was willing to obey what she felt God was calling her to do.

Perhaps it would be powerful for you to think back through your life: When have you *not* obeyed what God was calling you to do? And what might have been the impact of your disobedience?

What about right now? How is the voice speaking to you? What is God calling you to do? And what might be the impact you'll have because of some simple obedience?

It's Time to Talk Guerrilla

1. In Genesis 22:17–19, God makes a great promise to Abraham, and he says it's because Abraham obeyed. In Deuteronomy 6:3, God promises it will go well for his people *if* they obey. In Deuteronomy 28:1–2, God says he will abundantly bless his people if they fully obey.

2. So here's a question: is it possible that you're missing out on some of God's promises and blessings because you are not obeying him in some way?

3. In Deuteronomy 28:15 and 45, God tells his people that things will go very badly for them because they have disobeyed. So here's an uncomfortable question: is it possible that some of the things you really don't like about your life right now are a result of disobedience?

4. Read 1 Samuel 15:22. Do you think sometimes when you show up for church and make a "sacrifice" of praise or "sacrifice" some of your income to the offering, God is saying, "To obey is better than sacrifice," and really wants you to go home and just obey him?

5. Let's bring this obedience issue to being a guerrilla lover. Jesus said in John 14:15, "If you love me, you will obey what I command," and in John 14:23–24, "If anyone loves me, he will obey my teaching. My Father will love him, and we will come to him and make our home with him. He who does not love me will not obey my teaching."

6. Can you give some examples of Jesus teaching that we should live a guerrilla lover lifestyle?

7. If we don't really live as guerrilla lovers, we are not obeying Jesus. What does that say about us?

8. In what guerrilla lover way do you feel God calling you to obey him right now?

9. When will you obey him?

It's Time to Get Guerrilla

Sometimes what we need to simply obey God is accountability.

Yes, sometimes we're not sure what God is calling us to do. And perhaps sometimes we honestly don't have an opportunity to do what we want to do.

But most of the time we *choose* not to obey. We know what to do, we can do it if we want, but we don't want to, so we choose not to obey.

Even after reading this book, even after having your head filled with good challenges, even after coming up with some great ideas for doing guerrilla love, you quite possibly will not act on it and will remain unchanged.

Don't do it.

Perhaps what you need to obey God is accountability.

Why not loan this book to a trusted friend (or buy your friend a copy), ask them to read it fast, and then share with them what God is calling you to do. (Talk about living an everyday guerrilla lover lifestyle and about a specific challenge God has given you.) Ask your friend to keep you accountable. Set a date for when you will start engaging in the challenge. Develop a plan (if necessary) for how you will do it. Ask your friend to check in on you to make sure you don't back out, then go out and do it.

The impact you will have because of simple obedience will be significant.

So do it.

For more assignments and ideas, and to learn about and become a part of the Guerrilla Lover movement, go to www.guerrillalovers.com.

part 4

VICTORY

FLEAS WIN

Today I have to fly to Austin, Texas, and I'll be sitting in several airports. I promised myself I'd work on this chapter (the final chapter!), but I'm having trouble getting started. Okay, I'll be honest: I *can't* get started. And here's why.

I went through security and arrived at my gate to find out the flight is delayed. I'm going to be sitting here for over an hour. *That's okay*, I think. *More time to work on the final chapter!* So I find one of the few empty seats and sit down in front of a big flat-screen TV. It's showing golf, but immediately I realize something is up. Tiger Woods is playing, but I know Tiger Woods is injured and out for the year, so he *can't* be playing. I'm totally confused until a few minutes later when they break away from the action and an announcer comes on and explains that it is raining in Michigan, where the 2008 PGA Championship is supposed to be happening at Oakland Hills. During the rain delay the network is re-airing the dramatic 2000 PGA Championship. If the rain stops, they will go back to live coverage of the 2008 match.

Oh, that explains why Tiger Woods is playing and why he looks so much younger. What they're showing is from eight years ago.

They go back to showing the old golf championship, and I get out my computer. A guy comes huffing up to the gate, realizes we're delayed, finds the only seat left open, two to my right, and plops down into it. He starts watching golf.

I turn back to my computer to work on this chapter (the final chapter!), but I'm interrupted by a loud groan. It's the new guy sitting near me. I look up at the TV and see that Tiger Woods just missed a putt. And the new guy is *not* happy about it at all.

I go back to writing. Maybe I could use fleas as a metaphor . . .

"Oh crap!" new guy yells.

Tiger Woods just missed the fairway with his drive.

Okay, I totally know I should tell him that this is from eight years ago, but I can't. It's just too funny. This dude is so nervous, he's living and dying with every Woods stroke—oh, he just groaned again!—and I'm trying real hard to keep it together and not start laughing out loud at him.

It's hysterical. This guy is really worried about an outcome that has already been decided. Somehow he's completely into this but still is unaware that we already know who wins. Tiger will battle it out with Bob May, they will eventually have a three-hole playoff, May will miss a forty-foot birdie putt, and Woods will blast out of a bunker to two feet and make the easy putt for par to win on the final hole.

New guy has nothing to worry about and doesn't need to get upset over missed shots because the outcome is already decided. Tiger Woods wins. This guy just doesn't know it.

And I know the right thing is to tell him, but there's no way I'm going to do it. In fact, I'm praying that the flight gets delayed further—this is just too much fun.

♥

I'll tell you what's *not* always fun: being a guerrilla lover. In the interest of full disclosure, I just have to admit it. I've been following Jesus now for about eighteen years. For the last fourteen I've been in full-time ministry. And the truth is that loving and doing good and trying to help people can be tough.

Take what I've been doing lately, for example. I am in the process of trying to help four families that are imploding due to stupid choices. I'm doing everything I can to get them through this, I don't know if it's going to work, and honestly, it's emotionally exhausting.

We also have friends who just went from having zero kids to having *three* (having a baby and adopting twins in the same month), so tonight we're bringing over pizzas and hanging out with them because life is overwhelming for them right now. But I just got a text message from another friend, whose wife just had a miscarriage two days ago, and he asked if we could bring dinner and hang out at their house tonight because their pain is overwhelming.

I've seen things in these last few years that are so disturbing and revolting I would never put them down on paper.

I've poured into people only to see all the help I offered rejected and their lives go straight down the tubes.

And all of it really has an impact on me. So often I feel like all the good I'm trying to do is worthless, pointless. Like I'm losing, defeated.

Maybe you've been there. Or maybe you are there. Perhaps you've started trying to do good, to not live for yourself but for others. Perhaps you've started with a life of guerrilla love, but . . .

Already you've hit some road blocks.

Already you've stumbled.

Already you've felt emotionally, mentally, and spiritually drained.

Already you've been disappointed by the results.

Already you've felt like you were losing.

Well, if that's the case, I need to let you in on a little secret . . .

We've already won.

You may be groaning, you may be nervous, you may be living and dying with every result, but you don't need to be.

The outcome has already been decided.

You may be unaware of this, but we already know who wins.

In the end, God wins. We win. In the words of one pastor, love wins.

We still need to go out and live guerrilla, but we do it knowing that we already have the victory.

This makes me think of times in the Old Testament when God's people are forced to do battle with some enemy nation, and God tells them to go out and fight, but that he has already given them the victory.

God has told us to go out and love, but love already has the victory.

The feeling of defeat we sometimes have reminds me of the followers of Jesus when they watched their friend and hero be crucified. They stared with stunned faces, unable to speak. How could this happen? Jesus had lost. Love was defeated. They turned out to be on the losing side. But soon these followers discovered the reality of their situation, a reality that was always true, although they just couldn't see it. What they viewed as Jesus's greatest moment of defeat was actually his greatest moment of victory. In that moment, love had triumphed.

So often all we see are setbacks and disappointments, and we feel like we're losing, but the reality is that we have already won. The final chapter of this story has already been written, and we win.

♥

Now to that flea metaphor . . .

In 1970, Robert Taber wrote the book *The War of the Flea: How Guerrilla Fighters Could Win the World!* He compares guerrilla fighters to fleas. That's a great metaphor. Unfortunately, right now I hate it because our dog, Kuma, has fleas. We went out of town for two weeks and left our dog with another family, and when we picked him up, he had fleas. Rumor has it he hung out with another dog who may have been the source of the fleas, but I'm not sure if these rumors are believable since I read them on Kuma's MySpace page. What I do know is that these fleas are driving him crazy. He has become constantly fidgety, confused, disconcerted, and sometimes irate. These fleas are driving him crazy.

I've been trying to imagine what life is like for the fleas on Kuma. I've pictured a little sports reporter named Itchy Furman going down to interview the fleas in their locker room at halftime. They're all sitting around, getting some rest, drinking Flea-ade, when in walks Itchy, putting his tiny microphone into the fleas' faces.

"How do you think it's going out there?"

"Oh, Itchy, we are trouncing Kuma. We're eating his lunch out there, kind of literally."

"The surprising thing is that you started out as the under-dog—well, 'underdog' may not be the right choice of words here, but you know what I'm saying. I mean, this is a twenty-pound dog. I was reading in the team program that the biggest flea you have is 1/8 inch. With that kind of size discrepancy, how do you explain your success?"

"Dude, are you kidding? It helps us that we're small; this old bag of bones can't even see us. It's like, we're so small, how can he find us—and he's so big, how can we miss? Plus we're fast, and we can jump. And we've got the numbers on our side."

"So what's your strategy?"

"Oh, we're trying to drive him nuts. It's so much fun. I'll go down by the tail and start biting, and Dexter over there, he'll go up by his left ear and begin to nibble, and this stupid dog has no idea what to do. If his owners had any idea what's going through his brain, they'd put him in a straight jacket."

"Wow, very impressive. So are you enjoying this game?"

"Enjoying it? I'm loving life, Itchy. You know what I always say: it's a flea-eat-dog world. And it's a great thing to be on the winning team."

"But it's not over yet—you can't say that you're the winning team yet."

"Oh, trust me, we are the winning team. It's just a matter of time. In fact, I'd like to give my victory speech right now: I'd just like to thank the Lord, who made this all possible. And my mom . . ."

Do you think maybe the problem is that we've flipped God's script? Christians today somehow have the idea that we're the dog, but we're not—we're the fleas!

We pretty obviously think we're the dog. We talk about how we're a Christian nation and about the Judeo-Christian morality that is supposed to rule everyone's thinking and actions; we focus on how big and powerful we are. We think we're the dog, and if you think you're the dog, then you view anything that goes against you as fleas, and the fleas are infuriating!

But if you know that you're the fleas, well, then this world isn't enemy territory—it's your playground! You're the underdog, you have nothing to lose, and you've got this huge world you get to live in where you can jump around ambushing people with love left and right.

As fleas, we are agents of cognitive dissonance. Our goal is to drive people nuts: to live such different lives, lives so marked by love and joy and mercy and service that people are forced to question how they live their own lives.

And as fleas, we win. It's not over yet, but trust me, we are the winning team. We can give the victory speech now or later, but either way we know . . . the fleas win.

The outcome is already determined; that's no longer in question. The only question is, do you want to play on the winning team, or do you want to just watch?

My son and I are big baseball fans, and we are *huge* fans of the Los Angeles Dodgers. Back in April a friend of mine got us front-row tickets to a Dodgers game in Atlanta against the Braves. We sat with our feet up on the Dodgers dugout. It was awesome.

Now I want you to picture something: Let's say that the Dodgers were absolutely blowing out the Braves, so badly the Braves had no chance to come back and win. In the middle of the game the Dodgers' manager, Joe Torre, looks over at me and says, "Want to play?"

"Excuse me?"

"I'd like to give some players a rest," Torre explains. "There is no way we can lose this game, so would you like to play?"

Who in their right mind would say no to that? If there's nothing to fear—the outcome is already decided, so it's not like I could mess up and lose the game for my team—why in the world would I rather watch my team win than play on my team and be a part of the victory?

Of course I want to play!

Well, that's the question. Do you want to play? God has already secured victory for the guerrilla lovers. The outcome is decided. So do you want to watch the team win, or do you want to get out on the field and be a part of the victory?

Let's be honest: it's not exactly that simple. Because though it is true that God wins in the end, and it is amazing to get to take part in that victory, the truth (as I said before) is that being a guerrilla lover is not always fun and can be tiring and exhausting and overwhelming. Sometimes it's a real sacrifice to be on the team, but isn't it worth it? Isn't it worth the sacrifice to be on a winning team?

Did you hear about Trevor Wikre?[1] Trevor was a senior right guard on the football team for Division II Mesa State College in Grand Junction, Colorado. One day at practice Trevor felt something funny inside his right lineman's glove. It felt squishy. He assumed the athletic tape on his finger had come loose. But after the next play he took off his glove, revealing a shard of bone where his right pinkie used to be. The rest of his pinkie was hanging off. Wikre was taken to the hospital, where the orthopedic surgeon told him he'd need surgery. Trevor asked, "Can I practice tomorrow?"

The surgeon frowned and explained Trevor would need to recover for six months with no football. This would mean the end of Wikre's career.

Before the surgeon finished speaking, Wikre interrupted him, "Cut it off. It's just a pinkie."

The surgeon told him not to be dramatic; he would do no such thing.

Trevor told him to take the pinkie off already; he had a game on Saturday.

The surgeon questioned his wisdom again, and Trevor explained that his team was undefeated. "This team is too good, and there's too much love," he said.

The surgeon reluctantly acquiesced.

So Trevor Wikre will spend the rest of his life not being able to reach the p on his keyboard, and he'll never be able to pinkie swear or give a hang ten sign with his right hand, but if you talked to him, he'd tell you those are small sacrifices to be on a winning team.

And when you think about the sacrifices we may need to make—some exhaustion, occasional despair, some of our hard-earned money, a few people thinking we're crazy—really those are pretty insignificant prices to pay to be on the winning team.

In the end God wins, we win, love wins . . . the fleas win. That is the final chapter of the big story. But how will your story fit in the big story?

Have you heard of the book *Not Quite What I Was Planning: Six-Word Memoirs by Writers Famous and Obscure?* An online magazine asked readers to submit their life stories in just six words. It's actually an old idea. The challenge was given to Ernest Hemingway years ago to write his story using just six words. He retreated for a few weeks, then came back with, "For sale, baby shoes, never worn."

The online magazine received thousands of entries, which were later compiled into the book. A nine-year-old girl described her life with these six words: "Cursed with cancer, blessed with friends." One man wrote, "Seventy years, few tears, hairy ears." A woman wrote, "Followed rules, not dreams. Never again." One of my favorites: "Macular degeneration. Didn't see that coming." Some of the six-word memoirs made me sad: "Hiding in apartment. Knitting against depression," and "Not quite what I was planning." Others were humorous, "Lucky in love. Unlucky in metabolism," and "Born bald. Grew hair. Bald again."[2]

Whether you've thought of it this way or not, you are writing a story with your life. So what if you were to write a six-word memoir? What would it be? Or if someone else were to write it for you, what would you like them to say?

You still have time left, right? Your story isn't done. At the least you have the final chapter to write. And you're the one composing it. So what would you like your six-word memoir to be?

God is writing a big story in this world, and you are a part of that story, but how will your story fit in the big story? What do you want your life to be about? For what do you want to be remembered? How do you want to spend your few days here on earth?

If your life was a six-word memoir, what would you like your six-word memoir to be?

Maybe: *Guerrilla lover. Grace wholesaler. World changer.*

Or how about: *Loved unconditionally. Loved audaciously. Love wins.*

I hope mine will be something like: *Revolution called. Ambushed world. Fleas win.*

ACKNOWLEDGMENTS

God sent Jesus to bring a revolution. Jesus sent the Spirit to guide and empower his people to ambush the world with his guerrilla love. This book only exists because of God, and my deepest hope is that it brings him glory.

Thanks to Jen. You're my best friend and greatest supporter. You're also hot.

Thank you to Dawson and Marissa. You've helped me to understand and grow in God's love, and I hope I do the same for you.

Thank you to Forefront Church for giving me real-life examples of guerrilla lovers.

Thank you to Baker Books for taking a chance on me as an author and for letting me talk you into the idea for this book. I especially thank Chad Allen. Chad, you're a good friend and a great editor, and I'm thankful God has partnered us together.

Thanks to the people who read this book and helped make it better: Jen Sayre, Aaron Saufley, and Jennifer Antonucci.

NOTES

Chapter 3: Kingdom Come

1. Mark 1:15.

Chapter 4: Revolutionary Leader

1. Luke 11:38–40; see vv. 37–54.
2. See John 6:1–14, 22–66.
3. See Revelation 1:14–15.
4. See Revelation 1:16.
5. See Revelation 4:2; 14:2.
6. See Revelation 19:11–14.
7. See Revelation 19:15–16.

Chapter 5: Love March

1. John 4:3–4.
2. See Matthew 8:23–34.
3. Matthew 8:25.

Chapter 6: Revolutionary Creed

1. Mark 12:28.
2. Mark 12:29–31.
3. Mark 12:32–33.
4. Mark 12:34.

Chapter 7: Contagious Love

1. Luke 13:18–19.
2. See Mark 4:30–32.

Chapter 8: Guerrilla Lovefare

1. This story is told in Eusebius's *Ecclesiastical History* VII.22.

Chapter 9: Guerrilla Mercy-naries

1. See, for example, Matthew 5:43–44; Luke 6:27–30, 35; Romans 12:17–21; Colossians 3:12–13; 1 Thessalonians 5:15; and 1 Peter 3:8–9.

Chapter 10: Freedom Fighters

1. Yes, I did eventually get out. Otherwise I would have written this entire book in that stall, which would not be cool at all. How did I get out? I'm going to leave that to your imagination.

2. To verify that I don't make this stuff up, you can read this article at http://www.usatoday.com/news/nation/2008-03-12-woman-toilet_N.htm.

3. James A. Baker III, *The Politics of Diplomacy* (New York: Putnam, 1995), 172.

4. Pete Greig and Dave Roberts, *Red Moon Rising: How 24/7 Prayer Is Awakening a Generation* (Orlando: Relevant Books, 2005), 4.

5. Jeremiah 34:17, emphasis added.

6. Luke 4:18.

7. Shane Claiborne, *The Irresistible Revolution* (Grand Rapids: Zondervan, 2006), 232–36.

8. Barbara Brown Taylor, *Leaving Church: A Memoir of Faith* (New York: HarperSanFrancisco, 2006), 68.

Chapter 11: Kingdom Parties

1. See for example Matthew 8:10–11, 22, 25; Luke 12–15.

2. When our staff first started talking about the White Horse Pub as a potential meeting place, our youth pastor, James, was out of town. At our next staff meeting we jumped back into the middle of our ongoing conversation about the White Horse and whether it was something we should do. James sat with a confused look on his face until finally he asked, "Wait, are we talking about heroin?" (He's right, "white horse" is a slang word for heroin. I tell you this not to teach you drug slang but because it was really funny at the time. I guess you had to be there. But if you are reading this book to learn drug slang, I can help you with that too. "Firing the ack-ack gun" refers to a technique for smoking heroin by dipping the tip of a cigarette into it. So there you go. But please know that I am not encouraging you to fire the ack-ack gun but merely teaching you the slang in case, you know, you want the street cred or something.)

3. Steven G. Veigh, "Here, the Bartender and God Lend an Ear," *The Virginian-Pilot*, October 30, 2007.

4. See Luke 5:29.

Chapter 12: Radical Healers

1. You can find this story in Luke 7:11–17.
2. Luke 7:13.
3. Check out www.twloha.com.

Chapter 13: Wounded Soldiers

1. Thornton Wilder, *The Angels That Troubled the Waters* (New York: Longmans, Green, 1928).
2. Second Corinthians 12:9.
3. Second Corinthians 12: 9–10.
4. By the way, my favorite line from the radio station owner to Gerald is, "Your toot is inspired." That is classic!
5. First Corinthians 2:1–5.
6. Wilder, *The Angels That Troubled the Waters.*

Chapter 14: Anti-Terror Resources

1. You can find this story in Luke 12:13–21.
2. Luke 12:17.
3. Luke 12:19.
4. Luke 12:20.
5. Luke 12:21.
6. Andy Stanley, *It Came from Within: The Shocking Truth of What Lurks in the Heart* (Sisters, OR: Multnomah Publishers, 2006). Several of the ideas in this chapter are borrowed from chapter 15 of Stanley's great book.
7. Ibid., 166.
8. Acts 2:44–45.
9. Acts 4:32, 34–35.
10. David Workman, *The Outward-Focused Life: Becoming a Servant in a Serve-Me World* (Grand Rapids: Baker, 2008), 34–35.
11. Ibid., 35.
12. Ibid., 159.
13. Jim Robey, "Token of Kindness at Subway," *Dayton Daily News*, December 25, 2004.

Chapter 15: Lipstick Graffiti

1. www.banksy.co.uk.
2. John Burke, *Soul Revolution: How Imperfect People Become All God Intended* (Grand Rapids: Zondervan, 2008), 203.

Chapter 16: Subversive Service

1. Oswald Chambers, *My Utmost for His Highest* (Uhrichsville, OH: Barbour Books, 2006), 56.

Chapter 17: Covert Cells

1. See Victor Turner, *Dramas, Fields, and Metaphors: Symbolic Action in Human Society* (Ithaca, NY: Cornell University Press, 1975).
2. For more on this idea, see Alan Hirsch, *The Forgotten Ways: Reactivating the Missional Church* (Grand Rapids: Brazos, 2008), chapter 8.
3. Acts 4:32–35.

Chapter 18: Gas Molecules

1. See Matthew 13:45–46.
2. Shawn Day, "Oceanfront Preachers Deliver Message with an Attitude," *The Virginian-Pilot*, September 23, 2008.

Chapter 19: Worldwide Revolution

1. Mark 16:15.
2. Acts 1:8.
3. For security reasons, I will have to leave out the name of our people group and some other information in this story.
4. See www.compassion.com.
5. To make a loan to help lift someone out of poverty, go to www.kiva.com.
6. First Samuel 14:6.
7. First Samuel 14:8–10.
8. First Samuel 14:13.

Chapter 20: Revolutionary Risk

1. "A Victim Treats His Mugger Right," *Morning Edition*, National Public Radio, March 28, 2008, http://www.npr.org/templates/story/story.php?storyId=89164759.
2. I first heard this principle from my friend Craig Groeschel.
3. See Hebrews 11:6.
4. See 1 Samuel 17:26.
5. Quoted in Greig and Roberts, *Red Moon Rising*, 210–12.

Chapter 21: Lunatic Fringe

1. See Isaiah 20.
2. Ezekiel 4:1–15.
3. Isaiah 55:8–9.
4. Quoted in John Eldridge, *Walking with God: Talk to Him. Hear from Him. Really.* (Nashville: Thomas Nelson, 2008), 204.

Chapter 22: Insurgent Integration

1. Luke 10:29.
2. Luke 10:28.

Chapter 23: Simple Obedience

1. See Leviticus 18:4; Exodus 12:24; Deuteronomy 11:1; Matthew 19:17; and Leviticus 26:3.

2. See Deuteronomy 6:3; Luke 11:28; and John 14:15.

3. See John 14:21–23; 1 John 2:3–5; and 1 John 5:3.

4. Galatians 5:6.

Chapter 24: Fleas Win

1. Chris Ballard, "Digital Revolution," *Sports Illustrated*, October 20, 2008, 72.

2. Rachel Fershleiser and Larry Smith, eds., *Not Quite What I Was Planning: Six-Word Memoirs by Writers Famous and Obscure* (New York: Harper, 2008).

Vince Antonucci (Cincinnati Bible Seminary) is the founder and lead pastor of Verve, an innovative church plant for the unchurched on the Las Vegas strip. Vince's passion is creatively communicating biblical truth to help people find God, and he also serves with the Emerging Leadership Initiative (ELI). He is the author of *I Became a Christian and All I Got Was This Lousy T-Shirt*.

JOIN THE MOVEMENT

You can change the world with revolutionary compassion.
Meet other guerrilla lovers and join this growing social movement at

www.guerrillalovers.com

Find all the support you need to impact the world around you.

- Take on guerrilla lover assignments
- Share your guerrilla lover adventures
- Read guerrilla lover adventures
- Listen to guerrilla lover podcasts
- And more...

Are You Wearing the T-Shirt?

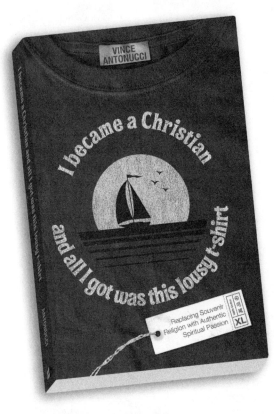

Many people find themselves asking, "Is this it?" Is that you?

Do you feel like you're missing out on the life God has for you? "We all read about the life Jesus describes and are painfully aware that our lives don't match his words," says Vince Antonucci in his first book, *I Became a Christian and All I Got Was This Lousy T-Shirt*.

Through provocative storytelling and raw honesty, Antonucci unearths the life Jesus lived and wants us to experience, challenging us to move past spiritual boredom into a faith that's exciting, beautiful, and powerful. Recommended for all Christians thirsty for a fresh perspective on Christianity. Pick up a copy today!

BakerBooks

a division of Baker Publishing Group
www.BakerBooks.com

Available wherever books are sold.